Eardisland:
Portrait of a Village

A photographic record of a historic heritage
by the Eardisland Oral History Group

Edited by Paul Selfe
Assisted by Cathy Dyer; John and Jenny Gittoes;
Brian and Tina Powell; Gill Richards;
Pat Roche and Jane Watson

Eardisland: Saxon Press
2006

ISBN 0-9526472-1-4

Published by Saxon Press
Brambledown, Lower Burton
Eardisland

Typeset and printed by
Print Plus
126 Widemarsh Street
Hereford
HR4 9HN

Portrait of a Village

This book has been compiled as a record of the heritage of the historic village of Eardisland. A cross section of the parish has been selected and photographs taken of all the properties, buildings and places of interest within it. Much of the changing social history of the village is revealed through these. We are grateful to everyone who has assisted us and provided information, suggestions and encouragement. We apologise to those whose properties we have omitted. We were unable to record every property in the parish and so for the purpose of this book, it has been divided into eight sectors, following the relevant grids on the OS map (Pathfinder 994). It may be that we can complete the research in a future publication.

The Sectored Map of Eardisland Parish

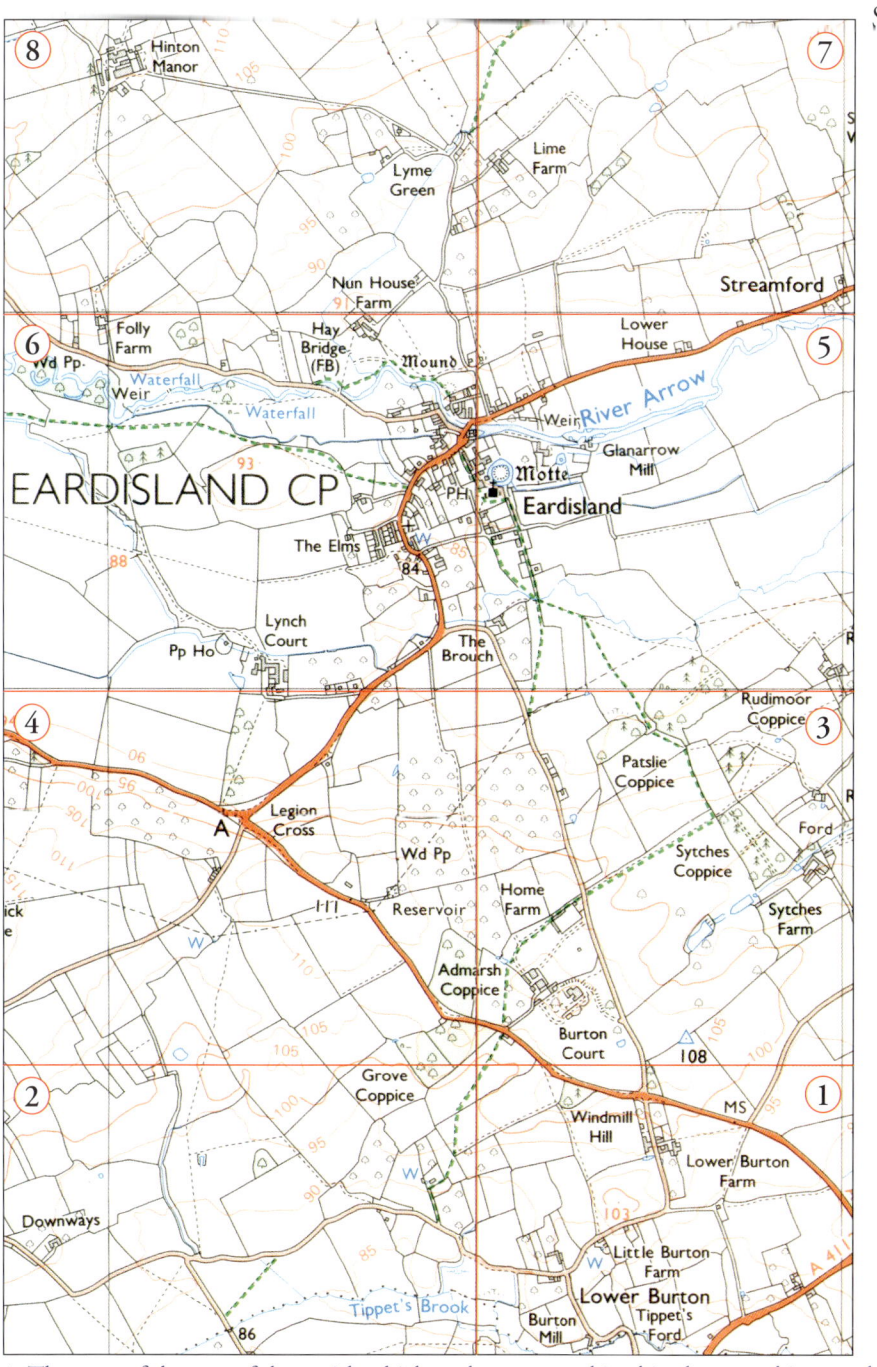

1. The map of the area of the parish which we have covered in this photographic record.

Contents

Dedication

Our book is dedicated to the community of Eardisland,
whose members have always given local historians
the greatest possible support and encouragement.

It has taken a long time to complete from the initial idea,
but we hope it will provide new information to residents and visitors
about the history and heritage of properties and places
of special importance in the parish.

The Settlement of Eardisland and Contemporary Social Life

The ancient history of Eardisland has been uncovered in comparatively recent times. Aerial photography (especially in the photographs of Chris Musson) has shown marks in the fields which indicate the presence of ring ditches, used to demarcate a funerary area. These may be of the Neolithic period (c.3000-2200BC) or the early Bronze Age (c.2300-1700BC). Some discoveries of flint and sherds of pot in these areas may be evidence for the fact that there was a settlement here from very early times.

In 2000 an Archaeological Projects Group (APG) was formed in Eardisland to undertake a case study of Burton Court and the immediate environment. One of the early major finds was a 'Dirk' dating from the Bronze Age. The blade was examined by an expert, Dr Martyn Barber, who suggests it originates to between 1400-1140BC. There is also evidence of later Roman habitation. A Roman Road forms the eastern boundary of the Parish. A number of finds dating between AD100-400 have been unearthed, including pottery and metal work in different parish sites. The work of the APG has also established a Norman presence at Burton Court. Among the important artefacts discovered are a large quantity of high status pottery, spinning whorls and the only gaming counter of the period so far found in Herefordshire.

There were at least four manors in the parish of Eardisland, (recorded from early post-conquest date); those of Burton, Hinton, Twyford and Eardisland itself. Whilst the present church building dates from 12th century, a church in Eardisland is mentioned in Domesday Book (1086) and may date from circa 950AD (although there is no archaeological evidence to support this). Eardisland does not appear by name in the Domesday Book (nor do Burton, Hinton and Twyford) but it is generally accepted that Eardisland is the second of the two places listed as "Lene" in this locality. The earliest of the black and white timber framed buildings have been dated from between 1350-1450. Others were erected in the centuries following.

Parish Population 1831-2001

Year	Ecclesiastical Parish	Civil parish
1831	791	Not known
1851	899	Not known
1861	894	Not known
1871	886	Not known
1881	781	Not known
1891	684	500
1901	679	470
1911	649	508
1921	643	496
1931	596	437
1951	597	463
1961	Not known	474
1971	Not known	439
1981	Not known	435
1991	Not known	444
2001	Not known	520

Data from Directories and also Reeves (p179)

NB: In 1884 Parts of the parish were removed; Bearwood was absorbed into Dilwyn and other outlying areas into Weobley. In the 1980s a small section in the north west corner was placed in Pembridge. Such boundary changes as have taken place make comparisons over time difficult.

The "Old Straight Track" in Eardisland

Alfred Watkins born in Hereford in 1865, was an early photographer and local historian. He wrote the The Old Straight Track (1925) in which he developed his theory that ancient trackways cut across Britain, in which hills, earthworks, churches and mottes are aligned along straight lines associated with the planetary system. He argues that the whole of Britain is covered in such trackways or 'ley lines' that connect such features. He suggests, speculatively, that they are examples of very ancient science. The problem is to know whether there is any true scientific basis to his theory (which he received in a "single flash" whilst crossing the hills near Bredwardine) and which has been criticised by archaeologists and scientists. Watkins says that "what really matters is whether it is a humanly designed fact, or an accidental occurrence …that mounds moats and beacons fall into straight lines throughout Britain…" However, for those intrigued or plain sceptical, the book does hold features of interest for Eardisland, in that he finds a specific ley line crossing the motte and moat.

The Motte and Moat

He describes it as "*A most convincing instance of a present day path aligning over a moated mound, its causeway, and an ancient ford with mark stone*". He says "*The flat*

2. The moated mound in about 1900

topped mound, within the moat is of considerable height from 15 feet to 30 feet." He describes the track as "*going past the school, sighted on the moat, also straight with the absolute precision of the causeway, which is on the other side of the mound to the path*". He goes on to explain that the ley goes over the Arrow and through Monks Court, where there is another small mound… "*Here the ley (exactly magnetic west) passes through one side of the mound about 4 yards from its edge.*" In addition, he makes other references to Eardisland in his study, where he found indications of actual tracks to one side of two barrows. His work may or may not have scientific justification but it makes interesting reading. There is one other speculation he makes with reference to Eardisland. He notes that there are four cross roads in the county with the name **Golden Cross** attached to them. He says that he had first surmised that these names marked the gold trader's track, for gold ornaments were prehistoric luxuries and gold was found in England and Wales. Interestingly, a map of 1865 marks the road that passes Burton Court as "*the Golden Valley*". But he says, two gold names were found on a ley through Arthur's Stone "*which is at the exact angle of sunrise on Midsummer's Day*". (He omitted to notice that there are two field names in the parish containing the word Gold, which perhaps did not fit his theory.)

Possible Neolithic flint finds

Assemblage of possible Neolithic worked flint, predominantly scrapers, were discovered in fields which aerial photographs show signs that they had a series of ancient ring ditches in them. This suggests that small groups were living in the area 4000–2000BC.

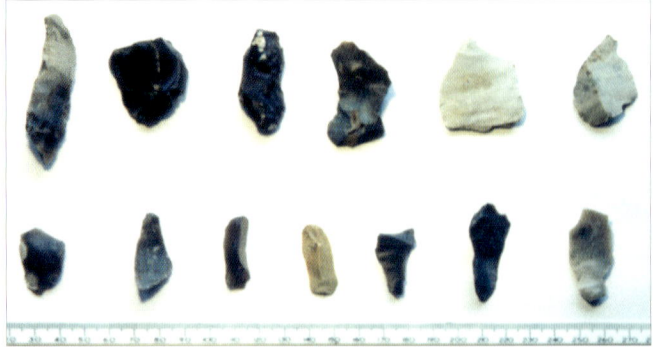

3. Assemblage of possible Neolithic worked flints

The Neolithic period in England sees the appearance of polished flint and stone axes, adzes and arrow heads and is generally associated with the introduction of cereal cultivation and animal domestication and the earliest production of pottery (*Arrow Valley, Herefordshire* ed. Keith Ray, p120).

The Bronze Age

The evidence of the existence of community dating to the bronze Age (3000 years ago) comes from the rare find of a Bronze Age dirk in the parish.

The Eardisland Dirk

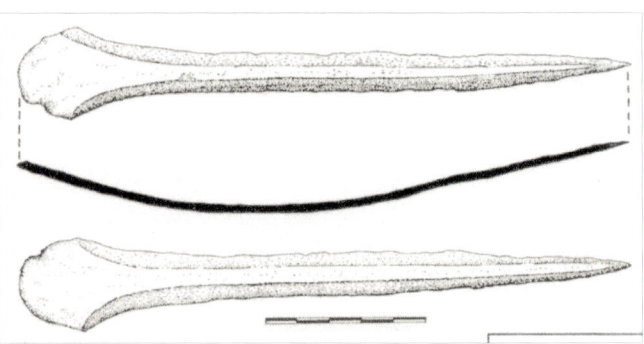

4. The dirk was discovered in 2002 close to Burton Court The drawing of the dirk is by Tim Hoverd (Herefordshire Archaeology)

The dirk was discovered in 2002 close to Burton Court. It is near complete. The metal is brown-bronze colour with green patches showing. It is defined as a dirk in terms of its length and shape (the blade is flattened or slightly rounded). It is thought to date from between 1400-1140BC. The nearest similar finds were in Swansea Bay and the Bath area. It is consequently a rare and important archaeological find which indicates the presence of Bronze Age people in this area.

[The photo is by permission of Hereford Archaeology.]

The Romans

A Roman road forms the eastern boundary of the parish and there have been finds of Roman brooches, pottery and other artefacts dating to the period 100-450AD.

Roman artefacts

5. Four fragments of Roman bronze brooches, a buckle and half of a medieval seal.

Four fragments of Roman bronze brooches (fibulae), include Dolphin and Trumpet designs. Some bear traces of enamel work. The buckle found in the same area, is difficult to date. Half a Papal Bulla (beneath the brooches) was also uncovered and is a medieval seal with religious connotations. 68 sherds of Roman pottery from another site in the parish have been identified as being Severn Valley ware which could have come from the Malvern Link kilns which were operating in the 2nd/3rd centuries, if not before and afterwards.

All these finds were made in 2004/05 in the parish.

The Saxons

After the end of the Roman occupation in about 450AD, the Saxon conquest began. In the course of the next 400 years their power spread throughout Britain. Hereford is believed to have been the headquarters of Saxon forces in their battles with the Welsh. It has been suggested that the name Eardisland derives from the Anglo-Saxon *Eardes*, meaning a dwelling place or home. B.C. Whitehead (WFC 1936, p53) says Merewald (who founded a monastery in Leominster in 658AD) divided the land in this area into three main portions, now called Kingsland, Eardisland and Monkland. On their outskirts grew up fringes of Anglo Welsh communities (such as Dilwyn). To defend these settlements earth works were dug to protect the inhabitants, animals and crops; the motte and moat in Eardisland served this purpose. There is no doubt that there was a Saxon presence in Eardisland and some of the pottery found in the excavation at Burton Court (2000-2005) has been dated to the late Saxon period,

prior to the Conquest by the Normans. Until the start of the Anglian occupation of this part of Herefordshire circa 600AD, there is largely no archaeological or documentary evidence. Thereafter, the Anglian invasion gradually moved westwards reaching what was to become Eardisland circa 700AD.

Sherds of medieval pot

6. Medieval pottery from Burton Court being sorted prior to identification

By the time of the Battle of Hastings, 1066, the lands in this vicinity were held by Morcar, Earl of Northumbria. The excavation on the mound behind Burton Court has unearthed more than 2000 pieces of medieval pottery, none later than the 12th century.

7. Medieval pot rims showing the large size of the cooking pots

Three basic types were identified. There was Worcester type ware; Malvern Chase fabric and Vale of Gloucester ware. This has produced the greatest assemblage of such pottery from anywhere in Herefordshire. The fact that it has come from some distance suggests it was for high status owners of Burton Court at the time of its use.

The Norman Gaming Counter

This may be the only such counter uncovered in Herefordshire and it was found in the mound site at

8.   A rare Norman Gaming counter found at Burton Court

Burton Court. Similar finds have been made in London and all date between 11th-12th century. They were Norman introductions. All are decorated on one face and embellished on the other with compass drawn grooves. It adds weight to the suggestion that a high status person was living at Burton Court in this period.

River Finds

9.   Two items found in the river in the village, of unknown date.

Eardisland Oak

Some of the huge oak trees still seen in the parish are thought to be over 500 years old. This is an ancient oak which is probably the largest in the parish. It is measured from time to time and is now 26 feet 3 inches round the trunk.

10.   The Eardisland Oak

Social changes

Whilst there are many such surviving features which represent the historic past associated with this village, there have been many social changes in the last 150 years which have resulted in the loss of some of its traditional past. Some buildings have been destroyed, (such as the old mill in the centre of the village and the workhouse, both of which burnt down), others became dilapidated in the days when property had much less value and were pulled down. The WI book of 1956 lists 21 as having suffered this fate before about 1855. Many other buildings have survived over centuries, but have changed their use. The old grammar school and the smithy, for example, have become owner occupied residences; the village school is now the village hall. At the same time there are many strong threads of continuity linking the parish to its earlier history. Large numbers of small cottages and barns have been extensively renovated, expanded and improved and some small estates of houses built.

Cider Making

Within living memory of many older residents cider was made by most farmers for their own family consumption and that of their workers. Cider apples were taken from their orchards in Autumn and crushed in the trough of the cider mill by a huge stone. In some cases this was turned by a pony harnessed to it. The crushed fruit was

11. The 18th century cider mill in Lynch Court examined by the Oral History Group

Hedge laying

14. A perfectly laid hedge in Lower Burton

then removed and placed between frames (covered in horse hair or hessian) one on top of the other and the juice squeezed out by compressing it beneath a powerful screw. The liquid was collected and put into barrels and allowed to ferment for several months before it was ready to drink.

There is still evidence of the old skills of cider making. A few cider mills remain in evidence; one in Lynch Court was operated by a horse and the ground was worn down by the constant circling process.

Cider Mill Stone

12. Smaller mill stones are now seen most frequently as garden ornaments

The process of crushing the apples to collect the juice more easily, is greatly assisted by the use of machines which can be towed by a car to any venue. The use of hessian covered frames remains a part of the process.

13. The modern way of crushing the apples by a mechanised system

Many old skills have been retained, even in the face of mechanisation. Hedge laying is still done by hand on some farms. The historian Norman Reeves records a conversation he had with an old farmer who told him that "*a 'superior' hedger ranked with the master ploughman and was a man of great value and intelligence. He not only had charge of all the pruning and plashings of hedges but also the planting of new ones. Only a large farm or estate would keep a 'superior'.*" It is recorded that in 1860 Joseph Arch and another hedge cutter earned an average of 4 shillings and sixpence (22p) a day for 12 days while performing a fencing contract on the Arkwright Estate (Hampton Court). The pay was well in excess of the average, but Arkwright said "*the pay was fair and the work well done.*"

15. Hedge laying in progress being filmed for the Oral History Group's heritage video (2005)

Floods

16. A serious flood in the village in the 1950s

Whether or not the village has always been susceptible to floods is a matter of debate. Barry Freeman (Parish Magazine 82, 2004) has argued that it depends how long "*always*" is. It may be that memories are based on the short term. In the run of history even 250 years is not long enough. In January 1769 a Wagoner with 5 horses were drowned at Eardisland. His boy on one of the horses was saved by clinging to a bough. In recent times the worst recalled floods occurred in 1929, 1947 and 1963. In 1947 following the severe winter, it was only the top of the bridge that wasn't under water and in the riverside shop the water was within two steps of the top of the stairs.

17. The Dovecote flooded in the 1990s prior to restoration

But if one takes the longer view and accepts that people were as intelligent in the past as they are today, it is unlikely that a settlement would have emerged around 700 AD in a place open to dangers from constant flooding. The river has always been essential for life. Water power ground their corn and fish provided protein. Water would have been managed in an annual cycle of river control to flood meadows when needed and to drive mill wheels. They would not have allowed the river to control their lives.

18. The Dovecote following restoration in more normal times

Village Customs, Traditions and Folklore

When the Oral History Group learned of the existence of a range of traditional customs and traditions associated with the village, it was decided to research and re-enact them and record them for posterity on a video. For example, there was a medieval prophecy that a battle would be won for the leader "*who shot the arrow first.*" This ambiguous prediction was claimed to have been proved by the victor, when prior to combat, the River Arrow was "shot" at a crossing point and the ensuing battle duly won. Owen Glyndwr was at the head of a movement that became a Welsh national rebellion, provoked by the oppressiveness of English rule. He had a major victory at Pilleth in June 1402 when he defeated Sir Edmund Mortimer, whose nephew had a claim to the English throne by descent from Lionel Duke of Clarence, 2nd son of King Edward 3rd. The personal combat between them (according to the historian R.H.George in a Woolhope Paper) is thought to have taken place subsequently in Eardisland. Glyndwr may have pursued the fleeing Mortimer and caught up with him at the point at which he was trying to cross the Arrow.

The Fiddler of Eardisland

19. Colin Cole made his own fiddles and played frequently in the White Swan

There are several customs which relate to Eardisland, which differ from those in other parts of the county. The willow was used in a custom to cure a child of illness by passing the young person between split boughs. In other parishes, an alder was normally used. There are stories of the supernatural and one in which a fiddler from Eardisland plays for dancers in Pembridge prior

20. Children, led by Gabrielle Hogg dance to Colin's fiddle for the re-enactment of the story of the 'Fiddler of Eardisland'

to a disastrous flood. When he returns for his gloves, the village has disappeared beneath the waters.

The Bull and the Cakes

In a Christmas custom, a bull was used to distribute bread or cake. These were placed on its horns; it was then prodded. If the cake was thrown into the stall it became the property of the owner, if it fell behind the bullock it belonged to the farm boys. A bucket of cider was then drunk and wassailing held, each one drinking the master's health.

21. The Bulls head, used in the re-enacted Christmas custom of distributing bread and cakes.

The Flaming Torch

Other traditions are concerned with the fertility of crops. In a New Year's Custom straw was attached to a high pole and a man selected to run with it, alight, over twelve lands of growing wheat. A land was the distance between sections of ploughed land. He would stop on the thirteenth and if it was still burning it was recognized as a good omen for the crop. Cider was drunk to celebrate the event.

22. The re-enactment of the crop fertility custom in which a flaming torch was carried across fields of growing crops

Blessing the apples

23. The apple orchards were blessed with cider in Springtime with a special ceremony.

Queen Anne's Bounty

Some fields in the parish are shown on the Tithe map as "*Queen Annes Bounty*". This was a customary tithe, imposed at the time of Queen Anne (about 1703) on certain fields. The funds raised went to the local vicar for repairs to the vicarage, the church or the poor. It was amalgamated into the Church Commissioners in the 1940s-50s.

Roping the wedding car

24. A wedding car seen in the 1950s with a rope preventing it from passing through.

In this custom, still practiced in the 1960s, children placed a rope across the road, near the church, to prevent the car from driving away. As soon as the groom had thrown some pennies to the waiting children, for good luck, it was allowed to pass on its way.

25. The filming of the 'roped wedding car' custom

New Traditions

26. The annual duck race attracts large crowds

There are new customs and traditions evolving which celebrate village life, in which the river plays an important role. There is an annual fund raising duck race.

The corridor of fire

In recent years the Leominster Morris men have visited the village at various times of year. They come to dance and celebrate the Midsummer, in a field in Broom Lane, with ceremonies of fire. This is followed by a celebration of the river, which has been such an important part of the history of the village, with dramatic candlelit model boats allowed to drift downstream at midnight. They also come to celebrate the cider apple harvest in orchards and maintain the tradition of wassailing in midwinter.

27. The Morris men celebrate midsummer at the River Festival with a corridor of fire

The Eardisland Cricket Bat

Since 1996, there is an annual cricket match between two village sides played for the Eardisland Bat

28. The trophy for the team winning the annual cricket match between the History X1 & the Howard Davies, Presidents X1, is the Eardisland Bat

When research showed that cricket had started in Eardisland in 1866, it was decided to celebrate 130 years of cricket in the village, in 1996. Two local teams played a match for the Eardisland Bat, provided by the Oral History Group. So successful was the event, that it has become an annual tradition ever since. The bat is presented to the winning captain, inscribed with the result, and it hangs for the year in the White Swan.

Social life in the village

Important Committees which act in the interests of the community include the PCC, the Parish Council, Millennium Fund, Dovecote Trust and the Village Hall. All these serve to bring the community together on regular occasions. They result in a strong shared sense of community values and identity and show that the parish remains vibrant in the 21st century. There are many clubs, societies and organisations which provide a range of opportunities and activities for local people to enjoy. They have the chance to become involved in bell ringing, art classes, flower arranging, WI, French conversation lessons, chess, oral history or archaeology. There is also a successful village band.

Eardisland's bell ringers have a long and impressive reputation, especially under the direction of the renowned expert, Leslie Evans (see also p28). He has been ringing from a very young age and has trained many people in the art and skills required. He has also repaired and hung bells in hundreds of churches throughout the country. The awards to the bell ringers are numerous and some can be seen in the belfry of the church, dating back to 1933. There are also teams that represent the village in rifle shooting, bowls, cricket, pool, quoits and darts.

29. The darts trophies on display in the White Swan

The Darts trophies include those for the winners of the Pairs Competition (2004/05), the Runners Up in both the Pembridge and Weobley Darts Leagues.

The village even has four successful international representatives.

The Village Internationals

30. Graham Simpson has represented Scotland at Archery for many years

31. Dick Preece has represented England at Quoits for several seasons

32. Katherine Thomas has been a regular member of the England Under 15 Rounders side 2004/05

33. Henry Simpson has been a member of the GB Australian Rules Football team and played in two World Cup competitions.

Eardisland in Bloom 2005

Eardisland won first prize in the Village Pride competition in 2004 and the Parish Council decided to accept an invitation to enter the Heart of England in Bloom competition in 2005. The pictures on these pages, taken by Chris Bivand in July 2005, show a selection of the public area features and private garden frontages which combined to make the village so much more attractive for both residents and visitors.

34. The Dovecote Garden
This delightful area was devised by Barry Freeman and funded by the Herefordshire Council and Eardisland Millennium Fund. The seats were made by Leslie Evans. The garden replaced what was formerly a wilderness of six feet tall weeds.

35. Further enhancement of the area around the Dovecote Heritage Centre has been provided by these planters which Diane and Chris Wolland keep well stocked throughout the season

36. Bridge Cottage is approached by a footbridge across the millstream and Lynn Ray created a most attractive waterside scene with flowers on the bridge and in the garden bordering the stream.

37. Eardisland Women's Institute funded the new rose bushes for the War Memorial garden to commemorate their 85th anniversary and the 60th anniversary of the ending of the second World War. The roses were planted by Graham Simpson

38. Liz and Paul Helme-Barnes make the frontage of the White Swan look so attractive with a mass of flowers in hanging baskets and tubs across their wide frontage.

39. At Shop House, Cathy and Malcolm Dyer have packed their front garden with flowers and the theme continues round the side with a flourishing buddleia.

40. The Burcott is a traditional timber framed house which Barbara and Ken Gill enhance with a wonderful floral display. Together with neighbour Jo Watson they also provided a floral display in the centre of the main street.

It is apparent that there is much evidence for the strong sense of community which exists in this village. The Village Show was reinstituted in July 2003, initially under the direction of Esther Simpson and has been running successfully each year since. The last one prior to this took place in 1956 when the first prize in the Draw was a live pig. The Open Gardens weekend was also revived in recent years, after the formation of the Millennium Fund Committee which was able to underwrite the costs of the event. This has also become another successful annual attraction for many visitors to the village in mid summer; the beneficiaries are the Village Hall and the Church.

Sector 1

Lower Burton: Windmill Hill to Burton Mill

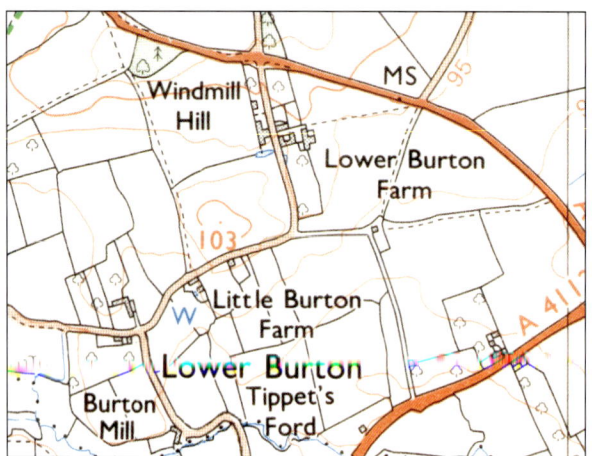

41. The map shows the area in which the properties appear in this section (1)

It is apparent from an examination of the Tithe map 1840/42 that the area known as Lower Burton is historically interesting. There is an ancient mill, (which operated until the war) fed by Tippets Brook; a common, (now a site of special scientific interest) and field patterns which show divisions into small units suggesting early medieval origin. Documentary evidence shows that they were all part of the Burton Court estate. They were traditionally within the manor of Burton (dating to the time of the Conquest) and most did not become detached from it until the death of Mrs Clowes in 1949 (whose family had owned it since 1862). Then, the estate was broken up and the tenants were able to purchase their properties. In addition, archaeological evidence and aerial photographs show many interesting features in some of the fields, suggesting that buildings or habitation systems of great antiquity once existed there.

Windmill Hill

42. Windmill Hill is one of the highest points in the parish

It is thought that windmills were always rare in Herefordshire. They were introduced from the continent from 12th century onwards. In 1778 Taylor shows only two on his map of Herefordshire. The remainder appear to have gone out of use by that date. The possible locations of such mills in this vicinity are suggested by names like Windmill Hill and Windmill Coppice. It has been speculated that the Round House, nearby, may have been connected to the site of a former windmill (although there may well be other explanations for the name).

Lower Burton Farm

43. An impressive 16th century building

The Royal Commission on Historical Monuments (RCHM), 1934 states that "*the house was built probably late in the 16th century on an L-shaped plan with the wings extending towards the West and South. The upper storey projects at the Southern end of the Southern wing on*

12

curved brackets. The barn, South East of the house is of three bays." In 1862, when part of the Burton Court estate, the tenant was Edward James and the farm comprised 264 acres. Thomas Davies was working the farm in 1901 (when he was also described as a cattle breeder and parish constable); but about the time of the first war, the Phillips family took it over and it remained in their hands until 1995. It was purchased by them in 1950 (the family also had connections with the Upper Mill), when the Burton Court estate was broken up. It was then described as "*the well known stock raising farm*". John Phillips described how when he was growing up in the 1920s, work on the farm started at 6.00am when the Waggoner came to feed and water the horses. At the end of his day ploughing with a one-furrow plough in the fields he returned to clean the animals down in the evening. It was said that if a man could plough one acre in a day he had done a lot of work. They had 20 working horses on the farm. "*As many as 50 head of cattle were walked to market, perhaps 20 miles and if they weren't sold they would be walked back…*"

Lower Burton Farm Knapp Orchard

44.   The site of a possible earlier moated farmhouse which awaits further investigation

45.   The ancient pond at Lower Burton farm

The field Kanpp Orchard contains evidence of ridge and furrow and a drainage system. Two platforms have been carved out suggesting they may have been the site of buildings subsequently abandoned. Large stones which may have been part of the building materials remain visible. There is also evidence of a track linking the site with other previously inhabited areas, including that in which the Bronze Age dirk was found.

Brambledown

46.   Two converted farm cottages which once housed workers for two separate farms

In 1858 when part of the Burton Court estate, this property (then known as Burton Cottage) was occupied by a member of the Trumper family, who farmed nearby fields as a smallholding of about 12 acres. In 1876, John Trumper was a bailiff and Miss Ann Trumper is described as a farmer. In the 20th century it had become two cottages, for the workers of two different farms and housed two large families. After 1950, one half was owned by John Phillips at Lower Burton Farm and the other by the Kington family in nearby Grove Farm. The water supply was a spring in a field about 100 yards distant. This was in use until 1995 (although then pumped electrically). One of the original cottages, which has timber framing, is thought to date from the 17th century. The other is probably a later Victorian addition. They had become dilapidated in the 1960s, and were renovated to form one house in the 1970s. Further additions were made in the 1990s.

47. Sunrise over Lower Burton

Laundry Cottage

48. Laundry Cottage in the 1990s before renovation

The original cottage is at least of the 18th century, although a deep finely constructed stone lined well recently uncovered in the garden suggests it may have very old origins, pre-dating its appearance on a map of 1833. In 1862, when part of the Burton Court estate, the occupier was William Pugh, a stone mason who held about 7 acres as a small holding. It was later used by the occupiers of Burton Court as a laundry. Older parishioners recall that a man would take baskets full of laundry in a trap on a Monday morning and return to collect it on a Thursday when it had all been washed and ironed.

49. The property has undergone significant reconstruction and renovation in 2004

50. Lower Burton at dusk

Little Burton

51. Little Burton is a mid 17th century property

This property is thought to have been built in the mid 17th century; the additional wing was built on in 1988, but with original materials. It was a smallholding worked by John Evans in 1934 and from about 1940 until the 1970s, William Nicholls was there. It was part of the Burton Court estate until 1950.

Little Burton Farm

52. Little Burton farm is an 18th century building

It is thought that a part of the house dates from about 1750 with a later addition from about 1825. William Jukes was farming there in the 1930s.

The Dairy

53. The owners of this cottage are among those who traditionally hold commoners rights on Pigmore Common

Burton Mill

54. Burton Mill is thought to date from 15th century

The earliest reference discovered is dated 1442 when John Mollesley paid 40 shillings rental for the Mill. It is mentioned in 1512 when Humphrey Cotes by deed settled on his son John and Eleanor his wife, "the manor of Burton with its Mill…". In 1858 the miller was William Parry and in 1865 it was Edward Edwards. In 1876 the miller was George Went, who is also described as "*a thrashing machine proprietor*". From 1900 until the mill ceased operations in the early 1940s, there were only four millers; George Symmonds, William Price, Edward Harris, and the last was Mr Hatton, whose son was killed in the first World War. It was primarily used for grinding animal feed, not for grinding wheat. The water came from Tippets Brook running through Pigmore Common. It collected in a pool at the back of the mill, where there were sluices which would have operated the flow of water to drive the wheel. Some of the original structures still exist, including the mechanical system which operated it.

Bridge over the Old Ford

Tippet's brook runs past Lower Burton Mill (being the southern boundary of the parish).

Interior of the Mill [Lower Burton]

55. Some of the original parts of the mechanism which drove the mill stones can still be seen in the barn section of the property.

Interior of Arrow Mill [Kingsland]

56. This shows the huge grinding stones used.

57. The old ford was bridged in the 1980s (below).

Sector 2

Pigmore to Downways

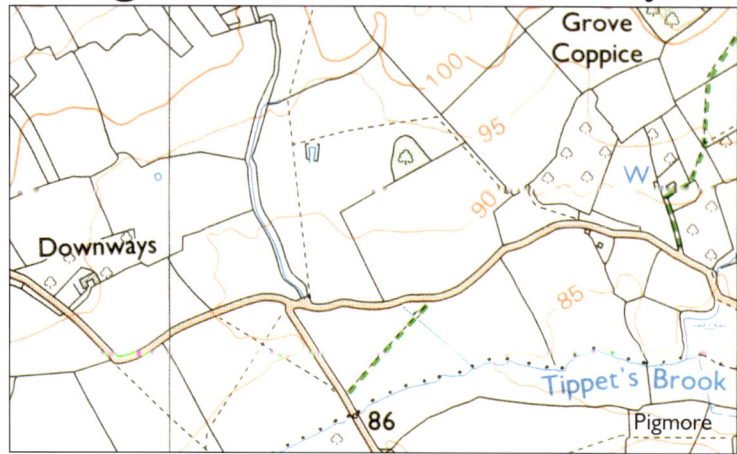

58. The map sector shows the area in which the properties appear in this section (2)

Pigmore Common

59. Pigmore Common is a Special Wildlife Site

On the tithe map (1840-42) it is known as Pigmoor Common; on recent maps it is written Pigmore. The origin of the name is uncertain. It is now designated a Special Wildlife Site by English Nature and contains important examples of plants and natural features such as yellow iris, water drop wort and various sedges. In 1967 commoners rights were registered, to ensure the quiet enjoyment of people of a designated area. These commoners included anyone living adjacent to the common or who had grazing requirements from nearby farms. Four were listed at that time. The rights are passed on with the property to subsequent owners.

The rights traditionally include
- Turbary (digging turf on the common)
- Piscary (fishing)
- Estovers (taking wood)
- Grazing (cheep, cattle and presumably pigs)

The Common Act 1899 establishes Byelaws which prohibit (without lawful right)
- Depositing rubbish
- Disfiguring any fence or notice
- Digging or cutting wood or turf
- Trapping or shooting animals
- Taking a cart or caravan across the common (including a photographic cart)
- Playing games
- Lighting fires
- Breaching the 1824 Vagrancy Act or doing anything which would adversely affect the land.

The bye-laws

60. The Common's Bye-Laws date from 1899

The penalty for breaching any Byelaw is "*a fine of 40 shillings*". It is not clear whether this has been increased in recent times.

In a memoir of school life in Eardisland in the 1850s, the author recalls that the quills used by pupils were collected from geese on Pigmore Common by a pupil who lived nearby.

The Round House

61. The Round House is close to Windmill Hill

Seaby & Smith in their survey of windmills report that "*well watered Herefordshire had very few windmills and for the centuries 1200-1700 we have none recorded. However, there is a Windmill Tump at Ley, Weobley and Windmill Hills are known… these could indicate windmills either in the medieval or renaissance periods.*". They note how in Worcestershire a windmill was converted into a house, in about 1900, which became known as the '*Round House*'.

It has been speculated that the Roundhouse, near Windmill Hill, may have been connected in some way to the site of a former windmill. It is a timber framed (square framing), two storey building. In 1862 when part of the Burton Court estate, it was the home of John Morris and his family, whose family members now extend to Queensland, Australia. He farmed about 12 acres as a smallholding.

Pigmore Cottage

62. Another cottage with close associations with Pigmore Common

Downways

63. Downway seen across the fields from Lower Burton lane

Downway or Downways (the deeds vary) was a smallholding of about seventeen acres until the 1930s. In 1858 it was the home of the Ricketts family, smallholders whose tomb stones can be seen in the churchyard. Several family members also farmed elsewhere in the parish. In 1901 Thomas Harris was the resident until about the time of the first war. In the 1920s Edward Cooke was there and in the 1930s Thomas George. In the 1940s it was farmed by members of the Hope family until 1947 when it was sold to Mr and Mrs Ernest Taylor of Oldham in Lancashire without the barn. They bought that later in 1959. Mr Taylor had a building firm and he got his men to demolish the old house and build a new one incorporating the farm building.

64. Downways was re-built in the 1950s

The barn, dated by an expert in timber framed buildings to the late 16th century, is original.

65. The barn is 16th century.

After the Taylor's deaths the property was bought in 1972, by Mr and Mrs Nute, veterinary surgeons in Leominster; then in 1977 it was purchased by Mr Frederick White of Parbold in Lancashire. There was a rare variety of apple growing in the orchard of this property, which thanks to the Marcher Apple Network, now has a sturdy fruit producing offshoot in their nursery in Talgarth. They have named it the 'Downway Costard'.

Sector 3

Burton Court to the New Cricket Ground

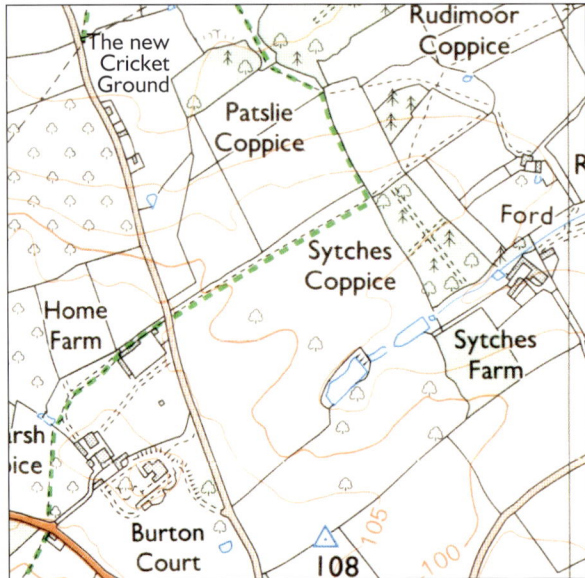

66. The map shows the area in which the properties appear in this section (3)

Burton Court

67. Burton Court 2005

A considerable amount of information is available about the families who were lords of Burton from earliest post-conquest date. It is believed that the first was Morcar, Earl of Northumbria who held (Earls) Lene (which would almost certainly have included Burton). In 1091 William 2nd gave lands (this specifically included Burton Court) in Herefordshire to William Braose. Manorial copyhold tenure and its surviving privileges were abolished by the Law of Property Act 1922. Col. P. L. Clowes (d. 1925) was therefore the last lord of the manor. The last recorded Court held at Burton was on Wednesday 17th March 1869, when John Clowes was lord. As to the building itself, archaeological work still on-going. The history of the building on the present site is in many respects still obscure. It seems possible that the very small amount of material surviving from an early stage of the Great Hall (expertly dated to the early 15th century), represents the first phase of building. After the early 15th century many phases of building of the present structure can be assumed, but not until the late 17th century is there any degree of certainty about the form and style of the building.

Dingley Drawing

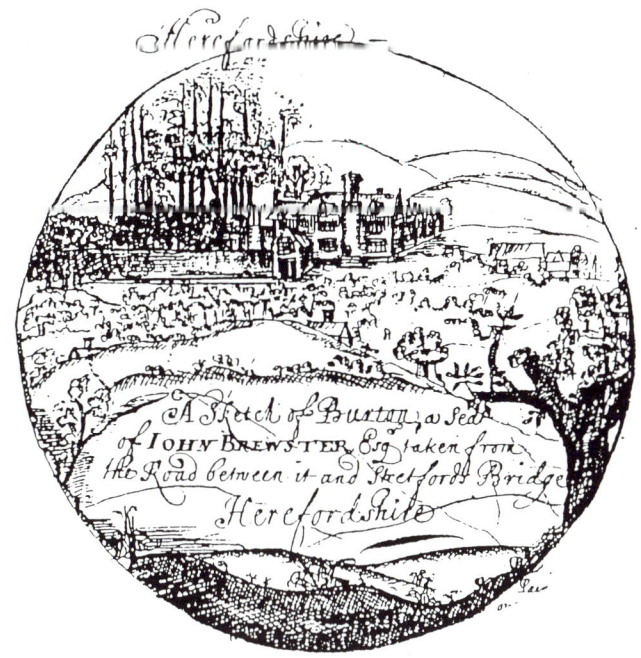

68. The Dingley drawing showing Burton Court in 1683

Dingley was a traveller and a diarist. His place of birth is not recorded. His father was also Thomas of the Southampton branch of the family. Several Manuscript Books of his various journeys survive. The one which contains the page showing Burton Court is in "*History from Marble*" (c.1683). It is possible that it provides an accurate view of the property at this time. An expert interpretation stated that it shows the upper residential range as a two storied wing of late 16th or early 17th century character, with its centrally positioned chimney stack. It was replaced in the early 19th century by the present dining room and kitchen extension. But the medieval range, approximately 26 feet wide extended at least 23 feet west of the Hall. The Hall and range formed two sides of a courtyard, now built over, but retaining the 72 foot deep well that has always served Burton Court. The gables have long disappeared since it has undergone many architectural changes over the years. Dingley died in Flanders in about 1695. From the Administration papers of his will it can be established that by then his home was in Dilwyn.

In about 1683 Thomas Dingley visited and made "*A sketch of Burton a Seat of John Brewster Esq. from the road between it and Stretford Bridge Herefordshire*". This sketch raises many more questions than it answers but it appears to show an Elizabethan mansion with five gable ends visible. The mound to the west of the house is also clearly there.

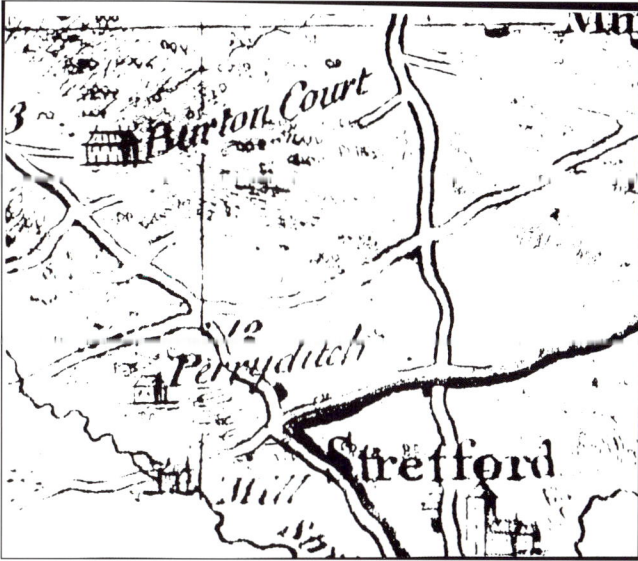

69. Taylor's Map showing Burton Court in 1748

The next view of Burton is on Taylor's Map of 1748. The general consensus is that Taylor did attempt to show different types of building as he actually saw them and was not simply using symbols; and so it can be said that at some stage in the 65 years since the Dingley sketch the gabled building Dingley shows was replaced by what can perhaps be described as a typical Queen Anne Mansion. Whilst there may well have been other building activity over the years, the next recorded alterations were carried out by the Evans family. Records mention that these were not completely finished in July 1837. The house was "Victorianised" by Kempson in 1865 and it was these "*…extensive alterations which brought to light a fine timber roof…*" This is the building which is to be seen in the earliest photographs.

70. A view of Burton Court in 1904

19

Then in 1912 a final spasm of alteration was carried out, predominantly, if not exclusively, to the east side of the house. The architect involved was Clough Williams Ellis and some photographs are extant of work in progress. There is no record of any work being done thereafter, although it must be said that, after the death of Colonel Clowes in 1925, there can be no doubt that his widow, Edith Emily Clowes, kept the property (and indeed the estate) in tip-top condition. Their only son, Warren Peter, was killed at the age of 20 in 1918; the estate was broken up and sold in 1950 following the death of Mrs Clowes.

71. The wall surrounding Burton Court has stones with the initials of past and present owners engraved on them

The present owners have provided wonderful historical exhibitions and teas with soft fruit available from the estate. It is presently being developed as a Conference Centre and for wedding use. A detailed history of Burton Court is being prepared by the Archaeological Projects Group.

The Poncelet Wheel

The pump house at Burton Court contains a Poncelet waterwheel which dates from the 1850s. Poncelet was a military engineer who fought with Napoleon. He invented the breast wheel which was more efficient than any that previously existed. The water enters about halfway up, rather than at the bottom or the top. However, it required a good head of water to operate, making it less useful in dry summers. The wheel has been put into operation at least once in the past 30 years.

A Lister Junior oil engine was used to pump the water to the house. When this was converted to electricity the oil engine was removed. It was salvaged by Stan Williams, (who lived in the village) and it was used for sawing wood. It is still in existence.

Home farm

This was built in about 1902 (and was first known as *Quebec* prior to the building of the present Quebec

72.   The Poncelet Wheel in the pump house

Cottage on the A44). It was part of the Burton Court estate and used by a senior employee of the Clowes family. The first occupant is thought to have been Henry Fielding, who was the farm Bailiff, and was there until about the time of the first war. Thomas Tebby was the last 'Farm Foreman' to Mrs Clowes.

73.   Home farm is an early 20th century property

Pigeon House near Burton Court

In 1389-90 the accounts of William Walsche, bailiff mention the *"hire of two carpenters for 15 and 16 days respectively at 3 pence per day, for repairing the bakery,*

74. The Pigeon House was once part of the Burton Court estate. This photograph was taken in 1934

76. The property was once part of the Burton Court estate

waynhous, dovecot and kitchen." The building collapsed in a gale in the early 1990s. This pigeon house is thought to have been part of some farm buildings, including the dairy (known as The Dairy House). When this was demolished (in about 1865) some of the timbers were used to build the Cricket Pavilion which stood under the lime tree in the old cricket meadow.

The first residents were the Watters family. Mr Watters had served with Colonel Clowes in the Boer war. He returned with him to become the coachman and later chauffeur to the Clowes family. He was sent to Yeovil to collect the car and learn to drive it. On his death the family subsequently moved into Lowcot.

Burton House

Keel Croft

75. Burton House is an early 20th building

This mock half timber property was originally named Highcot, and was the home of a senior employee at Burton Court. It was erected in 1903 for this purpose.

77. The roof level appears not to have been raised

This was originally named *Midcot* and in 1862 the tenant was Thomas Holland. It was part of the Burton Court estate and after the arrival of the Clowes family in that year, it became the residence of other of their employees. The Davies family was followed by the Sneads, a carpenter at the Court.

This property was re-named after the son of a previous owner who was a member of the Red Arrows acrobatic

78. This property is marked on the Tithe Map (1842)

team who was tragically killed whilst training. The property is interesting since it appears to have retained its original roof level, unlike the majority of other homes, in which they have been raised over time; (see for example Monks Cottage p78).

Old Pearmain (formerly Lowcot)

79. An 18th century property

The approximate date of construction is 1760. It is an excellent example of square panel timber framing of the period. Examination of the timbers indicates that a water-powered saw was used, a method favoured between about 1750-1820. Timbers in the roof are very rustic, some still have their original bark visible. It was probably extended to become a two storey building in the Victorian period. In 1861 prior to the purchase of Burton Court by John Clowes, the tenant was Joseph Williams. It then became known as *Lowcot*, when it was occupied by members of the Burton Court domestic staff. It was

sold off at the time of the death of Mrs Clowes, and the breaking up of the estate, between 1949/50.

80. This was the home of the butler at Burton Court in 1906

In 1906 the butler, Jack or John Hancox was living there with his family. He was obviously a blunt speaking man who once returned the hat of Colonel Clowes to him, having been admonished for failing to brush off some dust. He is reputed to have said that he could see no dust and if the Colonel could, he had better brush it off himself!

Plans of a house that was not built.

It is not clear where the cottage was to have been situated, but it may, perhaps, have been designed for Burton Lane, where a member of their staff might have lived. The plans were uncovered in Nottinghamshire archives.

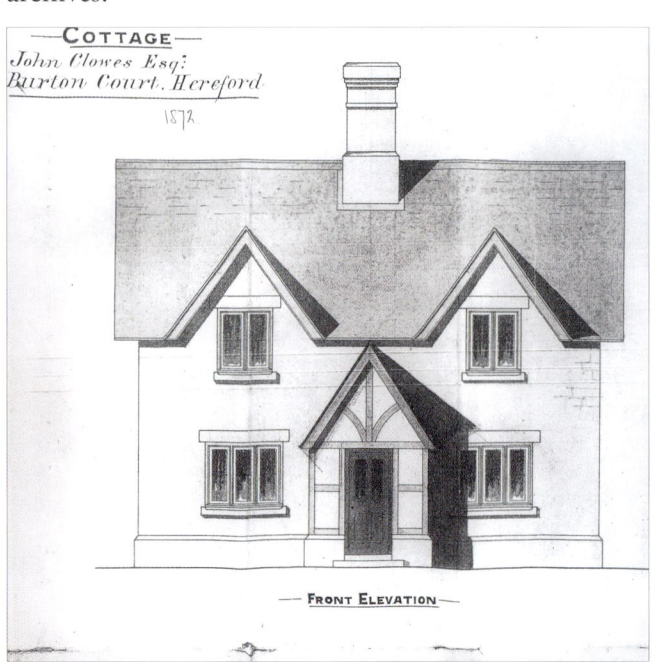

81. The detailed plans for a cottage commissioned by John Clowes (dated 20th March 1872). It is not thought to have been built.

Cricket ground

82. The Eardisland Cricket Club ground in Burton Lane (2005)

Cricket has been played on at least three grounds since 1866, when it is believed a club was first founded by Mr Leigh the schoolmaster of the time. It began on an old meadow in Burton Lane (see photo 110). It no longer served this purpose after 1939 when it was ploughed under wartime conditions. The post-war cricket club twice re-formed using the Nunhouse ground and then the present field, Southall's Meadow. This has again been used since 2002, when Mr and Mrs Edward Thomas kindly provided the opportunity to re-establish the Eardisland Cricket Club.

Members of the Cricket Club 2004

83. Members of the Cricket Club (2004)

Back row: Tom Hicks; Mark Hicks; James Weston; Paul Selfe;
Ben Woodcock; Alan Munn (Cpt)
Front row: Luke Jones; Callum Anderson; Zak Canning; Matti Jones;
Sam Gittoes; Greg Taylor.

84. The beautiful ground frequently attracts large numbers of spectators for matches

Sector 4
Quebec Cottage to Westgate

85. The map shows the area in which the properties appear in this section (4)

Quebec Cottage

86. This cottage is an early 20th century construction

Quebec Cottage has got an interesting history. A commemorative documents states that "*Edith, wife of Peter Legh Clowes of Burton Court, in the County of Hereford in the year of grace MDCCCCV11 (1907) did build this cottage to commemorate the glorious death and victory of Wolfe, her ancestor at Quebec MDCCL1X the tercentenary of the foundation of that city being celebrated in this present year. Col William Ellis and James P Scott of London architects James H Davies of Leominster, the builder. Carter Hopkins did first lodge here with wife and children September anno domini MDCCCCVIII;*". Wolfe: 1726-59.

In 1941 Thomas Parry was living there, but it subsequently became the home of Jack Hanson, who farmed locally.

Ding Hill

87. The property was built in 1928 to an award winning design in the 1927 Daily Mail Ideal Home Exhibition, by Mr Becker (of Lynch Court).

The first occupant was Miss Francis. Local historians are intrigued by the name Ding Hill. Recent researches by academic historians have suggested that the name Dingsmere in the *Anglo-Saxon Chronicle* (a contemporary history) may be related to the Old Norse for a place or assembly of Thing. The word would have been pronounced Ding by local people of the time. The researchers also note that Dingsmere derives from the old Norse for marshland of the Thing. The place name serving to warn travellers of the dangerous marshland in the area. (A paper explaining the theory has been published in The Journal of the English Place-Name Society). It is interesting that Ding Hill is close to Admarsh meadow in which a bronze age dirk was discovered in 2002. Furthermore, with Burton Court, close by, we may wonder whether it may have been the site of an Assembly in pre Conquest days. In addition, there is on the A465 near Ocle Pytchard, Thinghill Court; to the north there is Thinghill Grange and both are close to Sutton Marsh and Withington Marsh.

High Oaks

88.   Once one of the many small holdings in the parish

In 1905 George Davies was living in the property, which was one of the many village smallholdings, which have subsequently disappeared. It had about 18 acres and the owner would have been largely self sufficient. He was there until about the time of the first war. In the 1920s it was occupied by John Galliers and in the 1940s by Albert Postans.

Toll House and Turnpike roads

A toll house, with garden, stood at the cross roads of Legions Cross and another (perhaps smaller system, known as a Side Toll Bar) is thought to have stood near Tadpole bridge, to control traffic to Burton Court. There were two trusts (arrangements for the control and upkeep of roads) which served Eardisland, namely the Leominster (1728) and Kington (1756) trusts, whose jurisdiction met on Eardisland bridge. An Act to set up turnpikes for the improvement of roads through the area (including Eardisland) was passed in 1729. It was stated that "*these roads by reason of the deep soil and the heavy carriages passing through are become so ruinous and bad*

89.   A typical Toll House of the 19th century

that in the winter many parts are impassable for wagons, carriages, horses and other parts are dangerous for travellers." The upkeep of the roads came from the tithes and from those using the road, although the amounts were often inadequate. In 1854 the parish was indicted for not repairing a section of highway within its boundaries. It was the coming of the railway in 1857 and subsequent changes in local council structures and duties which put an end to the tolls and the toll houses. It is not certain when the ones in Eardisland disappeared, but probably well before the end of the 19th century.

Legion Cross

90.   Legion Cross was the site of the Toll House and the more recent AA Box

There is some doubt as to whether this name has a genuinely Roman connection. Reeves (p 186) says it may be a Saxon name. There is mention of 'Lidgeons Crosse Croft' in deeds of 1738; a map of 1817 (Price) shows 'Ridge Cross'; the 1832 OS map has 'Legion Cross'. Hence the name may be another case of spelling changing over time. However, before the road was widened, an AA Box stood on this crossroads until about 1955 (its telephone number was Pembridge 24). It is now to be seen beautifully renovated in the centre of the village outside the Cross public house. There were two AA men; the first Mr Williams used a bicycle and stood on duty by the box from 9am until 1pm. He returned an hour later and remained on duty until 6pm. On some days he cycled into Leominster and was on duty there. Mr Gittoes followed; he used a motorcycle to assist motorists in need of help. The AA Box on display in the centre of the village was rescued by Mr Harry Gittoes before the changes occurred nationwide to the boxes at the end of the 1950s. (See also p51)

Westgate

91. This property replaced one which was formerly the home of village centenarian, Florrie Jenkins

The medal won by Florrie Jenkins

92. The medal won by Florrie Jenkins in 1912

The original house on the site was built by Mr Prothero, who owned the White Swan, in 1900. It was lived in by Florrie Jenkins who died in 2002 aged 100. She received a silver medal from Sir James Rankin for 5 years unbroken attendance at the village school between 1907-1912. The present house was built in 1998.

The letter of congratulations was from Sir James Rankin. He wrote *"Dear Miss Jenkins, I have much pleasure in sending you his small reward for five years unbroken attendance at Eardisland School. I sincerely hope that this attention to regularity will be useful to you in after life and that you have been forming a character for regularity which will prove of great assistance to you. Wishing you a happy Christmas".* When she left school she duly obtained many interesting posts, acting as a personal ladies maid and later caring for children in families for whom she worked.

Sector 5

Lower Rhydimoor farm to the War Memorial

93. The map shows the area in which the properties appear in this section (5)

Lower Rhydimoor Farm 2005

94. A 16th century property which has been greatly renovated in recent years

95. The property seen in 1930s

The earliest reference found to Rhydimoor is 1508 in a bailiff's account which states *"certain meadows and pastures that were due to be sold at divers prices namely the meadow of Ridmore for 12 pence an acre."* In 1616 (29th June) it is stated in a sale agreement *"several parcels of land in Erdisland, including Rhyddymore"*.

This timber framed farmhouse is marked on Price's map of 1817 as Ridimoor. Aerial photographs show crop marks near the farm buildings, described as *"a complex of regular and irregular enclosures… often considered to show a British farm in the Roman period"*. The variations in the spelling of the name of this property provide an interesting example of how names change over time, in publications and on maps. In 1856 it becomes *Rhydemore*, when Edward Webb was the occupant. In 1865 it is recorded as *Rhydimoor*, when the farmer is James Perkins. In 1895, when the resident is John Sheen it becomes *Rudimoor*, although in 1905, under the same occupancy, it is spelt once more as *Rhydimoor*. Prior to the present ownership, occupants included William Ricketts and in the 1920s, William Downing. A final complication in the spelling is added by the fact that the OS map makers seen uncertain as to which is correct. Whilst the 1986 edition has it *Rhydimoor*, the Pathfinder 1989 reverts back to *Rudimoor*. The farm is situated off a roadway which is itself variously spelt as *Sytches* and *Stytches* lane.

The Brouch

96. There is much local social history associated with this property, especially in connection with the bells of the church.

The name may have derived from Brugges, bridge or crossing. In 1304 there is mention of "*Villa de Bruges*", which may refer to this property, being close to Tadpole Bridge. In 1339 the Burton Court Rolls record the existence of John Bruchford, perhaps an indication of the owner at that time. In more recent times there is reference to "Brutch Cottage" (1832), "Broaches" (1842) and Brooch (1885). Such spelling changes may reflect the transcription errors of clerks and map makers.

Leslie Evans

97. Leslie Evans, Captain of bells for more than 60 years

It has been the home of only two families since the middle of the nineteenth century to the present. The Parry family lived here for more than 40 years until 1923 and before them, the Jones family, who were also in residence for about 40 years. Since 1923 it has been the home of Leslie Evans. He was captain of the Eardisland Bells, for more than 60 years, until 2000, when he was 87. He is still ringing in 2005. His memoirs are soon to be published. There was once a Holy Thorn tree growing in the garden, which bloomed in January on 12th night. It was struck by lightening and killed in 1947. There are some rare cider apple trees in the orchard of this property which are used by Bulmers and Pembridge cider makers, Dunkertons.

Stephens Cottage

98. This is thought to be a 16th century building

The wattle and daub uncovered during the renovations indicates that the property may date from the 16th century. A William Stephens owned a freehold property in Eardisland in 1774, although the exact site is not certain. In 1862 the strip of land on which the house stands, running up the road, is detailed on plans as "*Stephens*". The 1881 census has a William Stephens living in a property on what seems likely to be the site.

The wall painting

99. The wall painting uncovered in Stephens Cottage

A particularly interesting feature within is an unusual wall painting which was uncovered during restoration in the 1960s. The 200 year old painting was discovered by Jim Taylor, who had lived in the village since 1914 and whose family ran a local building firm. The painting is confirmed by experts to be genuine. The medium which has been used is egg tempora. Colour pigments have been obtained from flower petals. It is not certain what the scene represents with what appears to be a lighthouse in the background. The suggestion that it may be of Kew Gardens has been discounted by local art expert Peter Glenn. The property has also been part of the Court House estate.

Downnome

100.

Rim-a-will

101.

Overbush

Jim Taylor who lived to the age of 95 and whose family set up a building firm in the village lived in Downnome, initially. Mrs M. E. Rimmer occupied Rim-a-will. The

102. These properties (100-102) were built after the last war.

owner of garages in Overton and Bush Bank retired to Overbush.

Tividale

103. A property with a strange Chinese connection

A memory of this property came from Adrian Bull whose grandparents Austin and Marion Rose bought Tividale (previously named Green Hayes) in 1946. In 1947 during the floods that followed the terrible winter, the water was more than two and a half feet deep in Church Lane. The cottage flooded in the two front rooms. Buses were replaced with ex- army lorries, with long bench seats for the passengers. On the death of Austin in 1947, Philip Powles pumped the organ played by Leslie Evans for his funeral. Austin was born in 1876. He trained at the Wesleyan College in Handsworth and became a missionary to China from 1899 and married his wife from England in Shanghai (during the Boxer rebellion). He later became an Anglican and was ordained in 1913. He was a translator to a Chinese battalion in France during the First World War. The property was later occupied by the Harvey family, on retiring as one of the village shop keepers. Mr Harvey had set up the cocoa concerts in the 1920s to provide funds for the cocoa given each day to the children in the school.

Church Cottage

104. This property was built in the early 19th century but was enlarged in 1989

In the 1920s it was the home of the Watters family. Their daughter Edie, who married Pat Smith, had a long spell as clerk to the parish council and became an assistant to Mrs Clowes. More recently it has been the home of Bill and Mary Blatchford. All these inhabitants have played an important role in the life of the village community with work they have done on its behalf.

The Old School/Village Hall

105. The school (seen on the left) was built by voluntary subscription in 1825 on land donated by Revd Canon Evans of Burton Court. It was enlarged in 1874

It superseded the old grammar school which was built in 1652, near the bridge. In 1855 the schoolmaster (Mr Bullock) was also postmaster, parish clerk and a shopkeeper. Soup was provided free twice a week. Mr Leigh was school teacher in 1867 and organised the drum and fife band and also the cricket club. The school was expanded in 1875, when Mr Haines was the teacher. The children paid 1penny a week (or 3pence a month "*if paid punctually in advance*") until about 1890. (Payment was not charged on more than two children).

In the 1860s there was a Dame School in Porch House (run by an unqualified lady teacher) and a separate school in the Dovecote (for about 12 girls). They also used the old Grammar School rooms for a while. But following the first national Education Act, which introduced compulsory education (although not fully enforced until 1880) boys and girls were both taught in this National School. In 1872 there were 26 girls on the register who were also taught in the building separately, by Mrs Leigh. In 1893 a new class room and cloak room was built (by voluntary subscription) when the official number in the school was 54. By 1875 integration had taken place. Mr Rogers was the teacher in charge between 1888 and 1901, after which Tom Wood took over. He was the Headmaster between 1901-1940. In his early years in the school, the numbers exceeded 100 on several occasions. He re-instituted daily hot drinks for children (funded by Mr Harvey's Cocoa Concerts); he was a noted sportsman, devoted churchman and worked to enhance the welfare of the local community.

Improvements to the school were made on a regular basis. A wash basin was installed in 1907, with a cloakroom and lavatory, (there were still earth closets in 1955) and electric light in 1931. Mrs Ann Davies was an assistant teacher in the school from 1912-1948 and like Tom Wood, is fondly remembered by many older residents. It became the Village Hall after the school closed through lack of sufficient numbers. They had declined from 57 in 1959 to 17 at the point of closure.

The school-room often served as a venue for village functions whilst it was a school. In 1872 there was "*a most interesting and instructive lecture given by Mr Ellwood of Leominster, entitled "An Hour with the Microscope", illustrated by the Magic lantern. The choir sang two glees and the entertainment ended with the usual singing of God Save the Queen*". In February 1920 a well attended meeting took place in the school room of the village *Fruit, Vegetable and Gardening Society*. Also in that month there was a visit of the Leominster Pierrots. In spite of bad weather the room was crowded "*really good songs were sung, genuine humour, absolutely unforced, kept everybody delighted from beginning to end.*" There were frequently held whist drives and dances. One in 1919 provided a range of prizes, including war savings certificates, a silver mounted scent bottle, silver cigar case, a pig, a duck and a brace of pheasants. In present times it is used on a regular basis by many village organisations for meetings, exhibitions and displays. In 1934 new rules were published for events held in the School Room.

1. MCs must be carefully chosen
2. In the event of any disorderly conduct it is the duty of the MC to report the offending parties to the managers
3. Gentlemen must not be allowed to dance together
4. Smoking by dancers whilst a dance is in progress is prohibited.

Since 1979 it remains the important venue for most village functions as the village hall. It is well used by many varied organisations and societies, under the auspices of a very active committee, which has never been obliged to enforce the 1934 rules.

Recreation Ground

This was previously the school playing field, provided by Mrs Clowes. On the break up of the Burton Court estate in 1950 it was purchased by Mr Harvey (of Bridge Stores) and subsequently handed over to the parish. Of the purchase price, £150 was raised by public subscription and £150 came from a local farmer. This

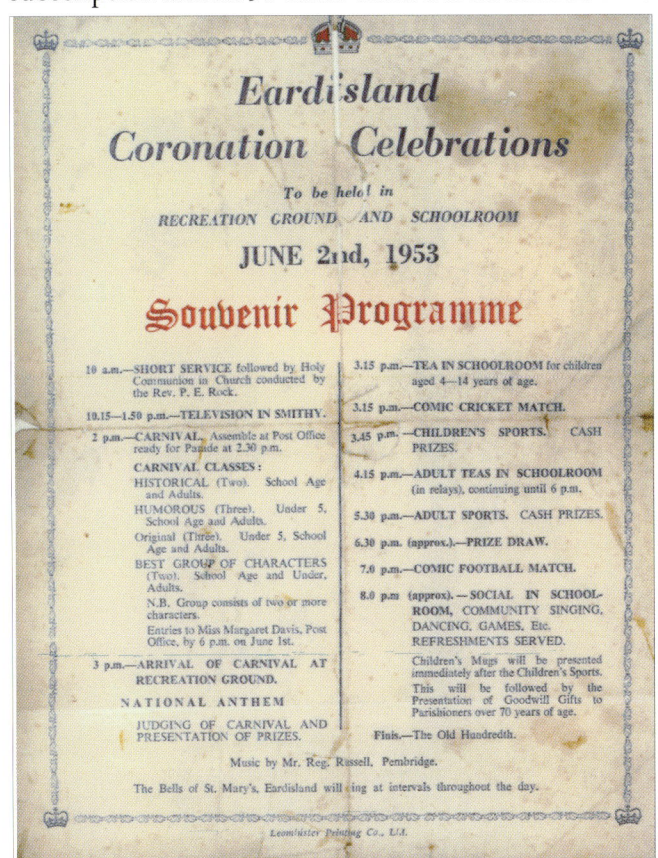

106. The Coronation 1953 was celebrated on the Recreation ground

has been a valuable asset to the youth of the village for many years. Mothers and Young Children make use of the play area; older children have an area for games. It is also used for annual village fetes. Many of the trees were planted to celebrate special national occasions, such as the Coronation, royal weddings and the Queen's Silver Jubilee.

School House

107. The School House is a late Victorian property

This was built in 1875 when the school was being expanded. It cost £208. Electric light was installed in 1931 at a cost of £9. The head teachers of the school lived there. The first was Mr Haynes, 1874-88; followed by Mr Rogers (1888-1901) and then Mr Wood (1901-1940).

Moat Cottage

108. This property is part of Court House estate and was built in the 1970s

Bowling Green

109. The Bowling Club has remained in existence without a break from about 1880 on three different sites

This is the third bowling green in the village. The first was sited on the Old Cricket Meadow and was shared with the tennis club from 1902. Mrs Clowes often presented the trophies to competition winners; she disapproved of women playing and especially of wearing shorts on the greens. The second was close to the river bank, on which Arrow Green now stands. This was paid for by Mr Price, who subsequently decided to build a house on the site. It was at this point, in about 1960, that the bowling green was moved to its present site. It remains one of the longest surviving village institutions.

Cricket was established in the village in the 1860s by the school master Mr Leigh; the Burton Court Cricket Club was instituted by John Clowes of Burton Court. The earliest known matches date from 1866. It is reported in 1872 that "*the ground is in capital order and with a pleasant change in the weather, practise has commenced regularly on Tuesdays and Saturdays at 6.00pm. The Club is in want of younger members to make more players, especially as regards bowlers; no subscriptions are taken this year from Eardislanders.*" The Club ceased to function after 1939 when the ground was ploughed up. However, a village club was re-established after the war but played on other grounds. A match was played in 1996 on the old cricket meadow to celebrate 130 years of cricket in the village.

A keen member of the Burton Court team in 1875 was George Yeld. He was born in 1845 (perhaps in Twyford, where the family lived) and died in 1938. He was educated in the Cathedral School, Hereford, went to Oxford, where following in the footsteps of Tennyson, Southey and Matthew Arnold, he won the Newdigate prize for English verse. He became a teacher and spent 52 years at St Peter's York. He was a mountaineer of great repute, edited the Alpine Journal and wrote books on climbing (including "The Mountains of Cogne"). He was held in high esteem by all who knew him and is described as "*geniality personified*" and "*incapable of making an enemy*".

Old Cricket Meadow 1904

110. A cricket match in progress in 1904 on the Old Cricket Meadow in Burton Lane

111. The meadow in 2004

Left scorecard:

Date August 21st 1875   18   Innings 1st Burton Court.
Match Burton Court v Hampton Court at Hampton

Order of going in	Striker	Figures as Scored	How Out	Bowler	Total
1	P.L. Llowes	22117221311321	bowled	Wyatt	32
2	J. Haynes	12	bowled ct Weare	Wyatt	3
3	J. Bruce	11	ct Hayes	Wyatt	2
4	G. Yeld	.	run out		0
5	P.J. Llowes	1	bowled	Hayes	1
6	B. Heywood	2121	bowled	Hayes	6
7	E. Child	3	bowled	Hayes	3
8	J.W. Guy	1111111	not out		7
9	W.J. Tivey	1	bowled	Hayes	1
10	J. Wrigglesworth	212111	bowled	Wyatt	8
11	J. Morgan	11	bowled	Wyatt	2
	Byes	11			2
	Leg Byes				
	Wide Balls	1111111111			10
	No Balls	0			0
					86

Runs at the fall of each Wicket: 1 for 42 · 2 for 40 · 3 for 41 · 4 for 57 · 5 for 57 · 6 for 53 · 7 for 61 · 8 for 68 · 9 for 75 · 10 for 86

Right scorecard:

Date August 21st 1875   Innings 2nd Burton Court
Match Burton Court v Hampton Court at Hampton

Order of going in	Striker	Figures as Scored	How Out	Bowler	Total
1	P.L. Llowes	1	bowled	Wyatt	1
2	W.B. Guy	1	bowled	Wyatt	1
3	J. Haynes	1	bowled	Wyatt	1
4	J. Preece	0	bowled	Wyatt	0
5	G. Yeld	151621	c Gordon	Hayes	14
6	P.J. Llowes		bowled	Wyatt	0
7	B. Heywood	1111	ct Heygate	Wyatt	4
8	E. Childe	0	ct Helme	Wyatt	0
9	W.J. Tivey	121	c & bowled	Wyatt	4
10	J. Wrigglesworth	12	ct Gordon	Hayes	3
11	J. Morgan	0	not out		0
	Byes	11			2
	Leg Byes	1			1
	Wide Balls	111111			5
	No Balls				
				Total	36

Runs at the fall of each Wicket: 1 for 4 · 2 for 6 · 3 for 6 · 4 for 6 · 6 for 23 · 7 for 25 · 8 for 25 · 9 for 36 · 10 for 36

112, 113. The score card of a match played 21st August 1875

In an account he wrote as an old man, entitled, *"The Story of an Old Cricketer: Memories of Matches from age 9 to 70"*, he provides a description of what it was like playing school and club cricket in the period 1854-1900. In his first village match he recalls *"I was very lucky, our adversaries came with one man short. So we agreed to play with 10 aside."* (How little things change). He writes, *"I got 8 wickets and put down the wicket of the 9th man who was run out. That made my local reputation"*. But the return match was a disaster. *"When we came to visit them the same villagers had their revenge for our team consisted largely of boys and we made only 9 runs, of which I contributed 6. The game remains with me because I caught and bowled their hardest hitting batsmen in both innings. In the first high up with my left hand and in the second high up with my right, my left was swollen very much, but sustained no serious hurt."* In another crucial village match he says *"we ascribed our defeat to the bowler who gave the enemy 5 wides"*.

He recalled some batting misfortunes. *"The following year I got very angry when a stout spectator sitting in front of the boundary railings at square leg, my favourite hit, prevented the ball from passing the fence by putting his hands in front of it instead of getting off his chair; I only got 2 instead of 4"*. He also noted that *"twice I have missed the 6 which a hard hit deserved because I had just made my partner run 6 from his own bat, which left him too exhausted to manage more than 5 for me, though my hit was better than his"*. He mentions in passing the mode of transport used in the days before motor cars and buses. *"In those days a long drive in a drag through smiling sunlit country was one of the usual delights"*. It is an interesting question as to how the Burton Court team travelled to away matches at Hampton Court and Leominster in the 1870s. On one occasion he recalls eminent spectators, the Bishop and his family, riding ahead in a large wagonette. Presumably the local train was used for more distant fixtures.

Tennis

114. Tennis in progress on the Old Cricket Meadow 1904

Also on the ground were tennis courts. A Tennis Club was started in 1886 and by 1888 had 50 members. It was still in existence in the 1920s, when members

115. A celebration on the meadow in 1902. Perhaps the Coronation of Edward 7th.

116. In 1996 a match was played on the Old Cricket Meadow for the first time since 1939. It celebrated 130 years of cricket in the village.

played every Wednesday afternoon until 7pm. It was finally wound up in 1936. A Football Club played on the ground from 1889 until 1939. Unfortunately, the Levick Cup, which was presented to the winners of the league, by Mr Levick of Eardisland, has disappeared. A Bowling Club made use of the tennis courts and was started in 1902. This continued until 1940 when it disbanded. It was subsequently reformed after the war and is now a well established and successful club on nearby land.

Wellcote

In 1792 the property, with lands and outbuildings attached, was occupied by William Dickens. In 1793 it is recorded that the Manor Court of Eardisland (Lord

117. This property was originally Well Cottage and has an interesting social history

of the Manor, Thomas, Marquis of Bath) was attended by Samuel Nash and Sarah Morris (his daughter, a widow) and Sarah Morris (her daughter) to whom it was let for life at four pence a year. In 1859, the Manor of Eardisland was under the care of J.E.Wilson and following a legal dispute, Sarah Morris was charged £20 and fifteen shillings for the property. In 1863 it was sold to Henry Tippins, for £50. He died in 1872 and left the property to his wife, Ellen. She died in 1881 and it was left to Esther Evans and Elizabeth Cresswell, of the Haven, Dilwyn. It was sold in 1895 to John Phillips, of Porch House (a blacksmith) for £15. (It seems that the property as by this time in "*a ruinous condition*"). It was then occupied by David Jones, but was sold 1897 to Revd Frederick Worsey and Mr King, of Dursley, for £110. In 1899 Mr King sold it to Revd Worsey for £55. In 1905 Revd. Worsey (vicar of Eardisland) died and left it to his wife Annie. She sold it to Fanny Jones of Church Road for £100. In 1917 she died and left it to Arthur Wallace Jones, a confectioner of Eign Street, Hereford. He sold it to in 1920 to Henry Gittins, of Court House, for £70. In 1927 Sarah Mainwaring was occupying the property at a rent of £1 two shillings and sixpence p.a. She purchased it in that year for £70. In 1952 it was sold for £400.

The Old Vicarage, Church Lane

118. The Vicarage was built in 1903. It is seen from the front in 2005

This property was built in 1903. The first occupant of the Old Vicarage was the Revd. F.W. Worsey (1902-05); followed by Revd. Richard Spencer Aldridge (1905-17). The Revd. Birley lived there between 1917-38. He was an Anglo Catholic. In this period the Guides and Brownies thrived under the direction of Mrs. Birley and met in the premises. She also ran a successful drama group in the village. The vicar had a full time gardener and two maids. The subsequent incumbents and residents were Revd. Rock, Rev Harmer and Revd.

119. It is seen here from the back garden in the 1930s.

120. Plans of a building dated 1842

Norse. When built in 1903 the site was purchased for £173 4.6. The cost of construction was £1850. The stable block was added in 1913 at a cost of £320. The SMR states that the design of the property owes much to the Arts and Crafts movement and was probably designed by J.Hartree (1869-1948); his house in Hereford (1900) indicates a building very much in the same character.

Before 1903 the Revd. J. Barker lived at Staick House which he purchased when he came in 1867. There was no vicarage house at the time, Littlebury's Directory (1867) suggests that this had been "*taken down about 40 years ago*". (This would give a date of 1827, plus or minus 15 years). There is documentary evidence to show that in 1367 a visiting Bishop Trillek discovered that the vicar of Eardisland had no garden in which to walk and grow a few herbs so he was provided with land from the rectorial glebe (Bishop Trillck's Register p. 252). It is believed that an earlier vicarage may have stood on Tithe Map Portion 547a (the kitchen garden of Staick House) in which the Revd. Frederick Rudge (vicar 1816-1867) was probably living prior to demolition. A Puritan survey of 1642 said the vicarage was worth £40 p.a. now vacant. "*The late vicar, Mr Bird, an old man, no preacher nor in his youth of good life. His curate Mr Barber, who sometimes preached is of ill report.*"

A vicarage that was never built

It is interesting to note that according to the plans of a building dated 1842 (perhaps the year that the vicarage on Staick House kitchen garden was demolished) there was an intention to build another vicarage. It does not appear that it was ever constructed although the plans exist in detail. They are described as "*Design for a Vicarage House*"

Viner Lodge

121. This property was built in the 1980s

Westwayes 1929

RCHM says "*Cottage, at the S.W. corner of the churchyard, has been heightened and extended towards the North*"; had they looked more closely they would have noticed three front door steps, each with "fancy" cobbles in front of them, which may indicate that it was once three dwellings. Recent expert interpretation has suggested that Westwayes is a high status early 16th century house with later additions. It is a two bay timber framed house laid out on a north-south axis to the south end of the present churchyard. A later timber framed bay has been added at the north end. The eaves level has been raised on both sides of the building. The later bay was added after the roof of the original two bays had been raised. On the ground floor the original two bays have beams with chamfers and well cut stops. The chimney stack at the south end is of brick and probably dates from the 18th or 19th century. There are carpenter's marks in the

122. The owner in 1929 peers from the doorway of Westwayes

123. A high status 16th century house

form of incised lines and circles. The fact that there are only two original bays may indicate that there was a separate kitchen or service accommodation. It could, however, mean that the building had some other function than purely domestic, especially in view of its proximity to the church and the possibility that it was once within a larger churchyard or maybe an area of glebe land. In 1929 the property was known as "*Church Cottage*", but by 1937 the Parochial Electors Roll detailed William and Mrs Iris Kendall as the inhabitants of "Westwayes". By 1951 he had died but she was still there.

The Church of St Mary the Virgin

124. In 1891 the church clock was erected by public subscription and wound by hand. In 2002 it was fully automated.

The Church (1950s)

125. Many of the headstones were removed from this section of the churchyard in the 1950s.

It has been suggested that Eardisland had a church in Anglo-Saxon times, but there is no archaeological or documentary evidence of this. However, in all the circumstances, it would not be at all surprising if there was. The first mention of a church in Eardisland is in 1086. The dedication to St Mary the Virgin is the same as that of several churches with which William Fitz Osbern is associated. Lyre Abbey in Normandy (now La Vieille-Lyre) was founded by him. The Abbey of Cormeilles (also associated with Eardisland in one Prime Source), 30 miles to the north west of Lyre, was also founded by this family. By 1067 Fitz Osbern had become Earl of Herefordshire and between then and his death in 1071 he gave the lands and tithes of the church at Eardisland "to Lire Abbey". Eventually, in 1415, Henry V added the lands and tithes of Lyre Abbey in England to Shene Priory, in Surrey, which he founded the previous year.

Of the church building which we know today the earliest parts date towards the end of the 12th century. Of this period are the (long ago blocked up) doorway in the south wall of the nave which was probably the priest's entrance to the then chancel. The doorway in the north wall is of the same date, as are both the north and south walls of the nave. This is evidenced by the three narrow "lancet" windows in the north wall, probably originally equally matched in the south wall where today only one survives.

The lancet windows

This feature is typical of the Early English Style, dating in this church from circa 1180. They were simple, small and unadorned to avoid making the structure of the building weaker, also to minimise draughts. In a later period some were replaced with more ornate windows filled with stone tracery.

126. These are so named because they form the shape of a little lance.

A number of the Parker family had military connections. In 1888 members of the Leominster Rifle Corps came to honour the memory of John Parker, killed at the age of 32 in an action which saved the life of a fellow officer. Two of his brothers had been soldiers and one, in the navy, had been killed in the South Pacific.

127. The Parker memorial window

128. Tomb slabs set in the floor of the Chancel

The east wall of the then building was where the chancel arch now is, in which there were a further three lancet

129. The 15th century screen when set in the Tower Arch, its third recorded position of four

130. Sedilia and Piscina in the south wall of the Chancel (14th century)

132. Memorial to Lieutenant Warren Peter Clowes, killed in action, aged 20

better served. Messages taken by him were always promptly carried with no regard for danger. No one could wish for a finer example or a better end to a blameless life". His commanding officer said "*he led his men in a most gallant way through very heavy artillery fire and fell just as he got to the trench. It was a very gallant death. Pat was the best we had; we all loved him so; to me his loss as a subaltern and a friend can never be replaced.*" (Wellington School, archive)

131. Three lancet windows.

windows with a round, or oval shaped window above them. There was (perhaps) a tower at the west end of this building. Over the centuries the tower has had its (architectural) ups and downs. The present structure is the result of work carried out in 1760. Of the 13th century is the doorway from the nave to the porch at the south-west corner of the building. What it replaced is not known.

The Warren Clowes Memorial

Lieutenant Warren Peter Clowes, Hussars, was killed on 30th March 1918. He had served with the 10th Reserve Regiment of Cavalry in Dublin during the time of the rebellion. He went to France in 1916. Brigadier-General 9th Cavalry Brigade wrote of him: "*I have never been*

133. Memorial to William Evans
(Lord of the Manor of Burton Court)

The 14th century saw a flurry of activity. All windows not already mentioned were then inserted (except the little square one, furthest east in the nave, which is possibly 16th century) and both tomb recesses (probably circa 1320); fragments of window glass; probably the tower; the porch (early 14th century); the vestry; the chancel (but only part of the roof) and in the chancel of the same period are the piscina, the three bay sedilia,

134. Doorway to vestry and possibly "Easter Sepulchre" in the north wall of the Chancel (14th century)

the arched recesses in the north wall and the external tomb recess in the south wall.

The Organ

In 1920, the old organ, dating from 1834 was sold to Lawrence Greenhough for £20. The existing instrument was erected by Messrs Wall, Norman & Beard. The case was built by Messrs Bridgeman & Son of Litchfield, to the design of Major H.B.Adderley of Warwickshire.

The present building suggests much less building activity in the 15th century. There is at least one fragment of 15th century glass. The north portion of the screen is 15th century, as is part of the chancel roof. The tie-beam, currently on the nave-side face of the east wall of the tower, is of the 15th century, (some sources say 16th century). Records indicate that the pulpit, font and lectern are all of the 19th century, and it was during that hundred year period that the Holy Water Stoup (immediately inside the door from the porch, on the south wall of the nave) was sawn in half to make room for an extra pew.

The 19th century pulpit

In 1851 the vicar was F. Rudge; Charles Scratchley was curate. In 1856 the living was in the gift of the Bishop of Worcester. Rev W. Harte was now the curate. Rev J. Powell MA was "*Head Master of the ancient grammar school endowed with £50p.a.*"

135. The organ was the gift of Col. & Mrs Clowes in memory of their son Warren Peter Clowes.

136. The 19th century pulpit is full of fine carving.

137. These drawing were made by the architect Mr Curzon.

The one on the left shows the church in a dilapidated state prior to alterations. The drawing on the right shows how it was intended to be. The keen-eyed will note several differences.

In 1863 an appeal was launched to cover the cost of an essential restoration, the building by then having become unsound, particularly the middle section of the south wall of the nave, and the roof of the nave. (The report stated that the Church had fallen into "a miserably and dangerous state of dilapidation". It added that "the bowl of the ancient font now stands in a cottager's garden".) These works were completed in 1864 resulting in the present building. Since then there have been no structural alterations, but many minor modifications to points of convenience to the interior have been introduced, for example, electric lighting and a heating system. Also, a re-covering of the roof of both the nave and much more recently, the chancel. The screen has recently made yet another move within the church, its present position being the fourth recorded.

The bells

138. The bells were re-installed in 1952

The church bells are of importance. An earlier peal of 5 bells was dated 1728, given by an anonymous lady parishioner and cast by Rudhall of Gloucester, said to be a replacement for an earlier peal. Drawings of about 1683 and 1712 show a spire on top of the tower.

Dingley's sketch

Dingley's sketch (see also Burton Court p19) shows the 15th century tower.

It may have been this which collapsed damaging the stonework on which it stood and the bells within the stone tower, causing the need for a new ring which was

139. Dingley's drawing

generously provided in 1728. In that year building work on the tower by Thomas Hooper of Yarpole cost £155. In 1832 it was reported that the passing of the Reform Bill was celebrated in Eardisland with great joy; there was a merry peal on the bells to accompany a procession of inhabitants with flags and placards. These were re-hung in 1906 with a new treble by the Whitechapel bell foundry being added. By 1950 they were in a bad state as a result of death watch beetle attack. They were taken down and recast with the addition of two new bells; the original treble was recast at the expense of the ringers whose names appear on it. The 5th commemorates the Coronation of Queen Elizabeth

140. The famous bell ringers of Eardisland and their successes commemorated

2nd; the 6th in memory of George Evans (of the Brouch) and the 7th in memory of the fallen in two World Wars; the tenor is in memory of Ellen Artindale of Glan Arrow. The new bells were installed with the assistance of Leslie Evans and local bell ringers and dedicated on 13th December 1952.

They have been rung regularly ever since, enjoying the reputation as the most perfect ring of bells in Herefordshire. Eardisland's bell ringers have a long and impressive reputation, especially under the direction of the renowned expert, Leslie Evans (see also p28) He has been ringing from a very young age and has trained many people in the art and skills required. He has also repaired and hung bells in hundreds of churches throughout the country. The awards to the bell ringers are numerous and some can be seen in the belfry of the church dating back to 1933.

141. Revd Nigella Tyson, Rector since 2000

Holmlea

The house is shown by RCHM on their plan of the village, but they do not include a description of it which means that it was not considered to date to before 1714. The earliest of the deeds of the property is dated 26th January 1771 and refers only to "Meadow Ground",

142. This 18th century building is the village Tea Rooms

no buildings. The first mention of a building comes in the Probate (dated 21st January 1824) of the Will of Mrs Sarah Preece "…to Minner (sic) Preece her daughter a house and garden." In the Will itself, dated 24th March 1823, the property is referred to both as a house and as a cottage. In a deed of 25th May 1818 the subject of the deed is still referred to as Meadow land and so the house/cottage was first built between 25th May 1818 and 24th March 1823. This property is the village tearooms.

Bardufoss

143. A property with war time associations

This property was built in 1965 by Reg Greene (whose son John founded Border Oak). It also initially housed a pet badger that lived beneath the building. The name has a wartime significance. Mr Greene was in the air force and whilst operating in Norway was hurriedly evacuated as the German army advanced. They were due to be shipped out from Bardufoss, but their ship was sunk and they had to wait there much longer until the replacement vessel arrived. The present owners moved into the house in October 1997.

The cottages in Church Road

These were erected in 1899 on the site of a previous row of old cottages.

144. These properties were erected in 1899 on the site of a row of older cottages

41

145. View from the rear gardens in Church Road

They were auctioned in 1920 when the rental was £39 and four shillings per annum and the tithe was one shilling and sixpence. It is believed they received the names Niche, Nutshell, Noggin, Nutmeg, Nook and Nest, from a subsequent owner.

146. The beautiful garden of one resident, Mr John Evans, has featured on a television programme.

91 St Mary's Walk

The properties, built in the late 1990s, are close to the site of an ancient monument (a moated motte) on which it is thought a castle or manor house may once have stood. They have been erected in what was previously a farmyard that belonged to Court House. An evaluation was conducted in 1990 to see whether the farmyard might have occupied the area of a castle bailey. The aim was to see whether any physical trace could be identified. The work was undertaken by a team from Birmingham University. The former causeway across the moat provided access to the motte from the farmyard, which suggested that this may have been the site of the bailey. This would have contained the Lord's Hall, a chapel, smithy, stables, barns and outbuildings. There was also an interest by the archaeologists in the unexplained dog-leg in the lane to the church as to whether it had significance as a line of a former rampart. The archaeologists divided the area on which the properties now stand into six zones, differentiated by

the character of the ground surface. Some trial trenches were dug and excavated. However, apart from a few Roman sherds of pottery, some medieval pieces of pot and some 18th century artefacts, there were few

147.

148.

149.

150.

significant finds. In fact, the quantity of finds was too small to enable features to be dated with confidence. From an archaeological point of view the results were inconclusive. However, the negative results cannot be taken as evidence of the absence of a bailey in this area, because of the small size of the excavated samples. Whilst the development of the properties was underway many medieval coins were subsequently found. It is prohibited to walk on the mound without permission and no excavations are allowed.

151.

152.

The Dairy (before renovation)

The Dairy (after renovation)

153.

154.

Threshing Barn (before renovation)

Threshing Barn (after renovation)

155.

156.

The Court House

157. There are deeds dating from 16th century which provide a detailed account of all owners and residents from that time.

On 23rd November 1577 it was purchased for £400 by William Whittington (who provided funds to build the neighbouring Grammar School in his will). The deeds *"reserved to the grantor, free access to one parcel of land of the premises called 'Old Hill Howse' for keeping the courts of the Leet there twice a year"*. (This house may have been situated on the motte, near the church). Then, following a series of legal disputes, it became the property of John Warde in 1627. He promptly sold it on to the Wall family, who owned properties in Pembridge and Lyonshall. In 1659 the Court House was purchased by Richard Dolphin for £1150. A suit was commenced in about 1670 against him because it was found that he was failing to observe the demands of a charity associated with the Court House. This entailed the distribution of 13 bushels of wheat and 13pence in silver to 13 boys of the parish. (However, it seems that the stipulations of the charity were still being enacted in 1891 when 13 bushels were distributed on Maundy Thursday.)

In 1727 Dolphin's widow left the estate to the Whitehead family. In 1742 it was conveyed to Mr Juson of Shrewsbury. It was acquired by Charles Haywood in 1785. There were a number of occupants during the later part of the 19th century. In 1858, Richard Watkins, in 1875 Josiah Coates, in 1885, Elizabeth Fencott, in 1898, Frederick Hope and in the early part of the 20th century, it was farmed by Edward Riley and later Henry Gittins. In 1934 the farmer was Douglas Powell and in the 1940s Christopher Morgan. The Clowes of Burton Court are thought to have owned the property and then the Arkwright family before it was acquired by the present owners in 1950. It remains a working farm, although the oast house kilns have not functioned for that purpose for at least 75 years. The building may also have served as a malt house and cider mill in earlier times.

158. The former oast house kilns

It is thought that Patience Strong lived in Court House, (which is close to the river), during the 1940s. Perhaps she was inspired by her immediate surroundings to write

"Rest your elbows on the bridge and gaze with quiet eyes… you will see… white swans moving in the reeds… little creepered cottages, round which the past still clings; here is peace untouched by all the clamour of our day, just a little river flowing gently on its way…stand upon an old grey bridge in quiet contemplation…"

The Fire

There was a fire in the Court House in 1889, which was reported in the local newspaper. The account describes the incident in great detail. On the night it occurred the property was occupied by Mr Thomas Price. Sometime after 11pm a young messenger was dispatched to Leominster on horse to raise the fire brigade. Once there, alarm bells were set ringing at about midnight, but only after the lad had been lifted over the huge iron gate on the market hall to get a bell rope. Firemen were ready quickly, but horses were delayed by 20 minutes as their harnesses could not be found. A fire engine was taken to the horses to save time and finally the team set off. At Buckfield, the four horses bolted. They were eventually brought under control at Barons Cross. After this delay, they got underway once more. But Cpt. Charles Moore allowed the horses too much speed down Ebnall Pitch. The fire engine pelted down the hill pushing the horses along with lack of control. Capt. Moore and the driver, Clayton, were thrown off together with assorted firemen, landing in the road, hedge and field. John Harris landed on his head but luckily he had his brass helmet on. Joseph Bowen and Thomas Evans landed on top of Superintendent Strangeward. Driver Clayton was found buried in a ditch in mud and slush, the soakage from a nearby smallholding, said to be somewhat smelly. Missing men were searched for with matches and a lantern from a nearby cottage. William Mann was sent back to Leominster for medical aid. Meanwhile, the horses careered on and cleverly turned right for Eardisland, but were finally stopped while trying to take a short cut through the hedges. Bemused firemen recovered the engine and eventually reached Eardisland in time to see the villagers themselves putting out the fire. Several firemen were put to bed. On hearing the sad tale, John Holman of the Royal Oak Hotel thereafter refused to house the fire engine any more as he considered it quite unsafe.

The Motte and Moat

There is no clear history of a building on the motte, although it is assumed that one must have existed. There is a record of William de Cantelope being ordered to "*arm the castle at Hordisland in 1213*", Robinson (1869) quotes Silas Taylor as mentioning that "*there is on the north side of ye churchyard an old moated hall which they call the Castle*". Some commentators have suggested it was the site of a Saxon stronghold, although there is no evidence for this. Rev Barker says of the mound in a Woolhope report "*this moated-mound is named on an old map of the Court House Farm, to which it belongs, 'The Fortress'*". A note in an early deed of the Court House refers to Old Hill Howse as the place in which the Court Leets were held. This could have been sited on the motte. In 1893 when the moat was cleaned out about 970 cubic yards of mud was laid in neighbouring fields, in which a few items of archaeological significance were later discovered. The distance round the moat was measured at about 190 paces. Present day ownership is shared by the residents of St. Mary's Walk.

Glan Arrow

Situated on the river bank, the existence of sluice gates with eel traps has been noted close by. In the 1860s it

162. This elegant property is thought to date from the 1840s.

was, for a while, the home of Benjamin Sanders (who was normally resident in Street Court). In 1900 Walter Williams was coachman to Cpt. Spencer, the then owner, and is reputed to have driven one of the first cars in the village. Cpt. Spencer could often be seen on his tricycle, followed by his dog, Ravishaw. It is recalled that he would shout to passers by to give him a hand to push him on his tricycle from one side of the bridge to the other. The Artindale family followed. The chauffeur became well known as 'Cabbie Williams' when he later ran a service to Kingsland Station. The Artindales were considered to be great benefactors to the village, providing assistance to many of the needy. They had three domestic staff and a gardener. After the last war it was the residence of the mother of Bruce Bainsfather, a wartime cartoonist, who devised the *Old Bill* character. Her son was a frequent visitor to the village.

161. The Motte (a mound forming the site of a castle) and moat. It is assumed a building existed although there is no hard evidence of this.

Glan Arrow Mill

163. Glan Arrow Mill fell into disrepair after about 1876

165. The mill was renovated to become a private residence in 1990s

164. The dilapidated mill in the 1950s

166. The beautifully renovated property in 2005

The Domesday book records two mills at Eardisland (see also Upper Mill). The earliest date at which its existence is actually inferred is 1469. It is possible that at one time (circa 1533) it was known as "*Curgit Mill*" but this is not certain. Until 1533 all references are to "*the Mills*" but after that date "Eardisland Mill" (Upper Mill) is separately referred to in documents (see p73). The other mill almost certainly was still operational, but by then not under the same jurisdiction as seems previously to have been the case. It is believed that Glan Arrow Mill was last in use as an operating mill in the 1870s when the miller was Charles Hundley. He lived in Glan Arrow Cottage, which no longer exists. The mill subsequently fell into disrepair and was subsequently renovated for residential use.

Staick House

It is thought that the name derives from Stank, meaning to dam. This may have been a crossing point of the river prior to the building of a bridge. The earliest part of the house is said to be the northern part of the east wing, which was built probably in the 14th century, as was one of the doorways in the east wall of the entrance hall.

A little later and probably late in the same century, the great hall was built as an independent timber-frame. The west wing was probably added in the second half of the 16th century. Late in the 16th century or early in the 17th, the hall was divided into two storeys and then the east wing was extended to the south about the middle of the 17th century. Late in that same century, or early

167. This is one of the oldest properties in the village and dates from 14th century. It is seen in a late Victorian photograph

168. Staick House in the 1920s

169. A contemporary view.

170. This photograph was taken in about 1890 and shows Revd and Mrs Barker with some of their children Joe, Rhoda, James and Jack

in the following one, the west wing was extended towards the north. It is believed to be the only house in the village which retains original windows.

It is thought the house continued as one dwelling until around 1800, when it was converted into four cottages. Lewis's Topographical Dictionary 1832/3, suggests that "*Staick House may once have been a religious establishment, a supposition strengthened by its peculiar appearance and contiguity to the Monks Court…*" There does not seem to be any supporting evidence for this view. In 1851 it is reported that "*Thomas Huxley was a tailor living in The Stank.*" In 1865, John Leigh, the Assistant Master in the grammar school lived there with his wife. The house was bought by the Reverend Barker soon after he came in 1867 and was restored by him in the early 1870s. The census of 1881 shows that there were 17 people living in the house on the day the information was collected. Revd and Mrs Barker had 7 daughters and 3 sons. There were 3 visitors (one from Prussia) and 2 servants.

Although he died in 1901 members of his family continued to live at Staick House until 1909, but the house by then was in a very dilapidated condition, and it was unoccupied and unwanted for three years until Mr E.J. Greenhough bought it in 1912. A programme of extensive repairs was undertaken in 1913 and indeed renovations of one kind or another have gone on ever since. The last major one being in 1950 when a new central chimney-stack was built and the roof restored, decayed oak being replaced and new stone slates laid. It was opened to the public occasionally in the 1960s. It is reputed to have one of the village ghosts. In 1914 a plot of land adjacent to Staick House (known as Vicarage Garden) was sold to Lawrence Greenhough. There is evidence to support the belief that this may have been the site of a vicarage which dated back to 1357 when the visiting bishop provided rectorial glebe for the vicar, it is likely that there was a vicarage on the site which was demolished sometime between 1842-45.

Riverside

This was the home of Jim Kington, in the early 1870s. He had been a soldier, fighting in the Crimean War, and he returned to farm in Eardisland. He moved to the Grove Farm in 1876, where the family then remained for almost 100 years.

This Victorian photograph shows Riverside in about 1890. This was owned by the Griffiths family in the

171. Riverside (previously known as Wayside and Roadside) seen in the 1890s

172. A contemporary view of the property

1920s who farmed surrounding land. On the death of his wife Edgar Griffiths donated funds for two additional church bells in memory of her.

Until the early 1900s this was known as Road Farm (with between 50-80 acres). It was once a small timber framed cottage, traces of which remain, but it has been renovated and changed over time.

The Granary

173. Serena and David Askew outside The Granary

This building is believed to date from the end of the Victorian period. It was once a working grain store One villager recalls grain being sold and carted away from what is now the kitchen window. It was converted into living accommodation in 1979-80

The Old Barn

174. Richard and Rita Kirby outside The Old Barn

This property is thought to have been built between 1750-1800. It incorporates Victorian church doors and some original stonework and timbers. In the memory of some villagers it was a working barn, in which sheep were sheared (until 1948) and cattle were housed. It was then owned by the Griffith family who lived at Riverside and farmed about 60 acres. It originally had double front doors (front and rear) wide enough to drive a tractor through. This barn conversion illustrates the changes which have taken place within the countryside over the past 50 years.

Bridle Goose

175. Thought to have been built in the late 17th. century and has an unusual original bread oven in the kitchen

The house has undergone a series of name changes. In 1936 it was Riverside Cott and in 1949 Stoneleigh, when it was occupied by the Atkins family. Later in the 1960s it received its present name.

Arrow Lea

176. Chris and Sue O'Grady outside Arrow Lea.

Documentary records indicate that the property dates from at least 1757 and possibly earlier (there are timber features which suggest this). New extensions have been added over the years and the barn was upgraded in 2003. There is a cider apple orchard behind. The occupants in the 1920s were members of the Emerson family; in the 1930-40s it was William Price. He was an ardent chapel man, through whose enterprise and efforts it was kept going until numbers declined in the 1960s. He also appears to have been the miller at Burton Mill between about 1910-30.

177. The garden at the back of Arrow Lea

The Dancing Tree Farm Shop

This is named after the unique hand carved wooden statue on display at the farm shop gallery. Extensive renovations have taken place during 2004. The tasteful interior design theme focuses on solid oak pillars and beams. The farm shop provides tea rooms, and various other shopping services to the community and visitors. It is the policy to support local producers and to provide customers with freshly picked farm grown vegetables and fruit.

178. The Dancing Tree Farm Shop continues in the agricultural traditions of the parish providing freshly grown produce

179. The unique hand carved wooden statue which gives the shop its name

Lower House

180. This property is marked on the tithe map 1840-42 and was one of the many village smallholdings.

Stonelea Cottage

181. A Victorian cottage

Swan Drift

182. The property dates from 17th century and has been subject to renovation in recent years

This beautiful house was originally a small black and white property, probably dating to the 17th century. Over the years it has been considerably expanded and renovated. The major development occurred during the 1950s. A cottage marked on the tithe map stood close by in an adjacent field. Roman artefacts have been found in the vicinity.

Staick Cottage

183. This provides another example of how the roof has been raised from its original level

In 1842 it was the home of Elizabeth Miles. Members of her family are still living in the parish.

In the early part of the 20th century, this was once the home of Staick House gardener, Charlie Thomas. He was also the miller in Upper Mill. Archie George, the village roadman (who is reputed to have kept the roads in the parish in excellent order, with verges neatly trimmed and ditches clean) was also an occupant of this property.

War Memorial

184. The War memorial soon after its erection in 1920. The area in which the trees are growing is now the village car park

This was designed by Cpt. A.B.W. Greenhough MC of the Staick House and executed by Messrs John Watkins & Sons Leominster. The cost was £208. This was raised by local subscriptions. It was dedicated on 14th March 1920 by Rev Birley. The land on which it stands was given by Mr Gittins of the Court House. The names on the memorial are those of: Ernest Morris; Rudolph Morris; George Roberts; Harry Smith; Harold Speke; William Webb; Peter Warren Clowes; Thomas Cook; John Davies; Stanley Hughes; William Jones; John Lewis; John Morgan; Donald Clayton; Stanley Farmer; and William Hatton. It is kept in immaculate condition by members of the local British Legion. (There are 114 names on the Eardisland Roll of Honour to be seen in the church, which commemorates all those who had been involved with the armed forces from the village).

185. The memorial in 2004

AA Box

After renovation

187. John Gittoes, son of the former AA man, Harry Gittoes, prepares for the opening ceremony in front of the renovated AA Box.

The work was undertaken by local craftsman, Roger Young and it was placed on public display in 2000. The exhibition in the Dovecote includes a rare 1920s patrolman's uniform, a walnut wall cabinet for AA members in appointed hotels (only two examples survive) and several rare signs, maps, handbooks, posters and keys.

186. This unique AA Box (perhaps the only one left in the country of this period) once stood at Legions Cross. It was stored in the garden of the AA Man when it became redundant. It is seen here in its dilapidated condition.

The AA Box is a unique survivor of Britain's motoring heritage. After the formation of the AA in 1905 the first boxes were erected in 1911. Later phones were installed. All pre-war boxes were replaced in the 1950s. The Eardisland box is the only known surviving example of the pre-war type of box. It stood at Legions Cross from about 1925 and was rescued by the local AA man Harry Gittoes and stored in his garden. Its significance was recognized following research by the Oral History Group and a restoration plan was devised.

188, 189. Visitors on the day the AA Box was again on view to the public in 2000

Sector 6

Lynch Court to Lime Cottage

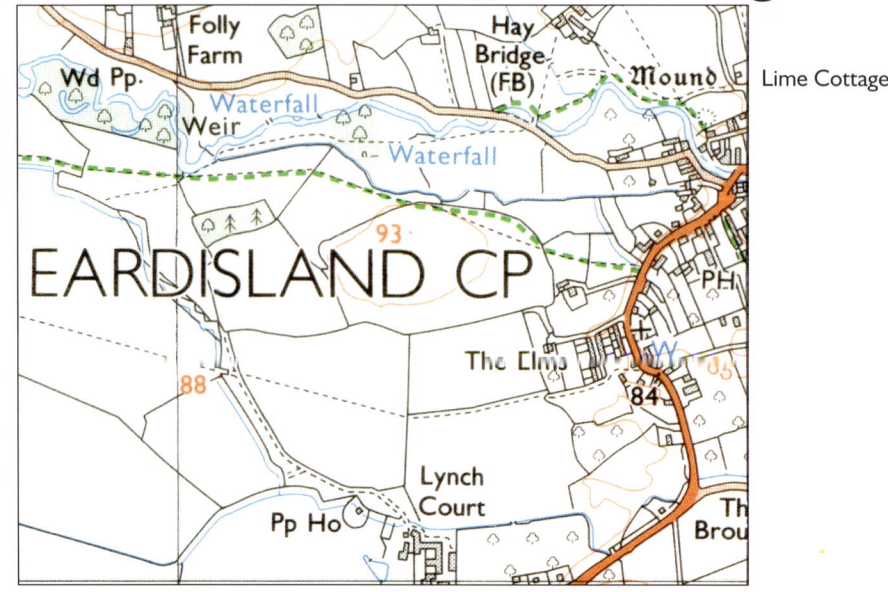

190. The map shows the area in which the properties appear in this section (6)

Lynch Court

191. In the early 19th century the Lady of the Manor of Eardisland lived in the property

Lynch does not appear in The Royal Commission on Historical Monuments of 1934. This was compiled to include monuments "…*from the earliest time to the year 1714…*" suggesting that opinion then was that the present building does not date from earlier than 1714, although a less grand edifice may have pre-dated it. The earliest reference we have uncovered to the Lynch is 1612. It is recorded that on 8th July, Richard Kynnersley of Eardisland, gent. signed an Indenture to purchase

various plots of land including… "*pasture of 20 acres called the Lynch.*" Then on 30th September 1696 another Indenture mentions "*Richard Kinnersley of the Lynch, Eardisland*" who leased "*his tenement called the Lynch, a messuage with 2 orchards and garden 20 acres of pasture*" From these two items it can be established that a house at Lynch was first built some time between 1612 and 1696 (perhaps nearer the latter than the former because on a map dated 1748 Lynch ("*Lyenck*") is still shown denoting an area of land rather than a dwelling.

The Kinnersley family were again living in the property between 1712-98. Their status is also noted by the fact that in August 1736 they were granted Pew No 1 in the church. In 1804 Elizabeth Kinnersley was lady of the Manor of Eardisland. In 1841 J.R.Smithies of Lynch Court wrote a letter to Hereford Journal telling of his experiments with "*Italian rag grass*" which he says "*to sheep farmers is the most valuable plant that has been introduced into England since the Swedish turnip.*" In 1865 William Turner was living in the property and in 1901 William Evans was in residence. In the early twentieth century it was occupied by William Evans and his family, who were there until about the time of the first war. In the 1920s it was occupied by Henry Jones, and from the 1930s, by Mr Becker and his family.

As to the place name "*Lynch*" the authority Ekwall suggests it derives from old English for "*hill*". Another suggestion is that it may have a Welsh derivation, from pond or (conversely) ridge or bank. The historian, Norman Reeves notes that the term Lynchets describes ancient cultivation terraces such as those on the hill near the priory in Stoke Prior called Paradise. These may have been for vine cultivation but the dating of lynchets is uncertain. Reeves also outlines in his notebook, details provided to him by a local farmer in 1976 (then aged 78) who said that there were some significant stones at the Lynch. He explained that a farmer would put a few strands of corn on his stone when he had completed harvesting so that villagers would know that the field was available for grazing. The stone's size was related to the acreage of the farm. Such stones were in Long Meadow, possibly extending from the Court House Pembridge. The grand country house had a large cider mill, worked by a horse or pony in which older residents recall large quantities of cider being prepared (see p5). The property has undergone renovations in recent years.

Roselyn

192.

Cherry Lyn

193.

Bramlyn

194. Each of these properties was formerly part of the Lynch Court estate. Cherry Lyn was built in 1948. The other properties built at about the same time were all used by family members or those employed at the Lynch.

Tadpole Cottage 1930s

195. This cottage was part of the Lynch Court Estate.

196. Tadpole Cottage 2005

This cottage was part of the Lynch Court estate and was for some time in the 1930s the home of the Cole family. Colin was a renowned fiddle player who frequently entertained at village functions (see also p7).

It is recorded that Quoits was played on the wide verge between Tadpole Bridge and Lynch Court in the evenings and Sunday mornings, with cider and beer for refreshment. The quoits were iron rings about ten inches in diameter and were pitched into a bed of clay about four feet square with a peg standing in the middle.

Orchard Cottages

197. Two early 20th century cottages.

These were built in about 1912-14 by the Clowes and are thought to be of "*Irish design*" since the Clowes had strong Irish connections. They were originally occupied by the Waggoner and the gardener from the estate.

Orchard Cottage

198. This was originally a small black and white cottage

199. Orchard Cottage in about 1900

This was originally a small black and white cottage probably dating from mid 17th century, which has been greatly renovated and beautifully improved in recent times. It was auctioned in May 1947 and described then as "*a picturesque half-timbered cottage*"; it offered "*living room, large pantry, two bedrooms, back kitchen, wash house, coal and wood shed and a pigs cot*". It had "*a good garden and a pump water supply*". The drainage rate was eleven shillings and two pence. The most recent additions took place between 1947-60, and again in 1993. Several important books have been written in this house by the late Gabriel Allington, most recently '*St Thomas of Hereford*', '*Hereford Mappa Mundi*' and '*Borderlands*'. These provide great insights into aspects of local Herefordshire history.

The Bramleys

200. This property was built in the late 1990s.

Brick Cottage

201. Once two small cottages which have been extensively renovated to form one property.

In the 1920s one was occupied by Andrew Powell, the Sexton and gardener at the Vicarage. The other was occupied by Tom Drew, who was one of the two roadmen for the parish, who kept the local highways in such exceptional condition.

West End Farm

202. This property was probably built in the mid 18th century

The house is shown by RCHM on their plan of the village, but they do not include a description of it which means that it was not considered to date from before 1714. The first map on which it is shown quite distinctively is the 1832 Ordnance Survey. Eardisland Manor Court records mention a property existing there in a document dated Wednesday 26th October 1757. In the 1920s Ernest Parry and his sister Hilda lived in the cottage next door. She took on the post of assistant overseer, collector of taxes and clerk to the parish council. She was taken twice a year by Mrs Evans of the Brouch in her licensed trap, to pay the taxes to the appropriate office. From the 1930s until recent times it was the home of the Smith family who were dealers and distributors of local apples. The Smith family had lived in West End until very recent times and had a long history and association with Eardisland. This was traced back through the Roberts family. John Roberts was gardener to Revd. Barker and it was John who planted the fir trees on the river bank by the bridge.

203. The old Fruit Depot.

The Sycamore West End

204. A new village property.

This property is still under construction as part of a long term project and is being carefully built with traditional materials.

White Cottage

205. Constructed in the 1930s.

The Latchetts

206.

55

207. A beautiful and typically English village cottage, thought to date from between 1650-1700

The thatch is "wrap over" rather than "saddle ridge". A thatcher's needle can be seen on the south gable. The gable end reveals that the roof was raised at some point. Early plans show that a privy stood in what is now the north east corner of the garden of White Cottage. There is a capped well in the front of the property. Additions were made to it in 2000.

Ruscote

It is a three-bay, timber framed cottage laid out on a north south axis. The north end is a slightly later (17th century) addition. In the central bay is a ceiling beam with wide chamfers and the frames at each end of the bay are faced up into it, which indicates it was a public area. The work in the beams is of high quality. The fire-place in the east wall is probably original. By the front door, on the west side, is a well which was still used in the 1960s. This may indicate that the bay closest to it, was the service (or kitchen end) of the property. Ruscote was the home of the village AA man who saved the AA box from demolition in the 1950s. This has now been restored and can be seen in the village car park.

208. The diagonal bracing in the gable ends of the building suggest that this beautiful thatched house was built in the late 16th century

Orchard farm

209.

New House

210. From the 1940s Orchard Farm it was the home of the Weir family and their smallholding business. Tom Weir had been Waggoner at Lynch Court. New House is a recent addition.

56

Green Elms

211.

215. Doug Powell in his immaculate garden

212.

216.

213. Pat Roche seen outside her house

217. Dora Preece and her son Dick outside her home

These properties were built as council houses in 1952. The first occupants took possession in October 1953. At present 12 of the 19 properties are privately owned.

214.

Green Lane Cottage

218.

The Haven

219.

220. Liz and Roy Harbour outside their home

The Willows

221.

Victoria House

222.

Holmleigh

223.

Apart from Green Lane Cottage, most of the properties in Green Lane have been built since 1960.

The Wesleyan Chapel

224. This chapel was built in 1864 and served the community for just over 100 years

It had seating for 150 people. At the back was a stable. Wesley wrote in his diary in 1746 of a journey from Leominster to Kington in which he passed through Eardisland. By 1875 there was a resident minister, the Revd Blackmore, who lived in the village in Arrow Lawn. In the mid 20th century Mr Harvey (the shop keeper of Bridge Stores) was the resident organist. There were two services on a Sunday and attendances were between 30-40. There was also a Sunday School. By the 1950s membership was down to three. Services ceased in the 1970s. It was finally sold in 1984.

Lynch Cottages

225. These were once part of the Lynch Court estate, in which employees were housed, including the under Waggoner at Lynch Court, Harry Owens

Garden Cottage

226. A Victorian cottage once the home of champion ploughman James Williams, who refused the opportunity to use a tractor.

The property was probably built between 1845-1870. In 1871 Elizabeth Charlotte Tomkins purchased it when it consisted of two cottages and gardens, (described as being "on the south side of the turnpike road") for £40. She also owned other adjacent land and buildings. In 1912 her seven cottages and orchard land (including Garden Cottage) were sold for £160 to William Henry Robinson of Kingsland. (It is likely that two of the properties she owned were the former workhouse, which closed in the 1840s). In 1912 the cottages were occupied by William Davies, Thomas Derry, Ellen Lloyd, Jane Owens, John Matthews, A. Leveson and one was empty. In that year Robinson sold five of the cottages to a Miss Stephens. In November 1918 he sold the remaining two cottages (now one dwelling, Garden Cottage) to James Williams of Arrow Cottage, for £105. (He raised a mortgage of £80 from Eliza Moore of Sparkbrook, which was duly discharged in 1944). He was a renowned ploughman, having won over 40 prizes (the last one a veteran's award, when he was 73). He worked for many years at the Lynch and never used a tractor. In 1944 Garden Cottage became the property of his son Stan Williams and subsequently that of his great nephew David Gittoes.

Stan Williams worked on local estates and was the village barber, cycle repair man and the source of much village memorabilia of important social history. Recent additions to the property were made in 2003.

The Workhouse

227. These cottages stood in front of Garden Cottage and were thought to have burnt down before 1920

It had been a place for the poor until about 1842. In 1761 when Thomas Owen took a House for the Poor he was paid £6 six shillings for taking them for a year. (Even in 1637 there were 41 names, mainly of whole families, receiving poor relief; this probably included at least 140 people, a quarter of the parish.) *"At a vestry meeting on 22nd February 1781 it was agreed that Mr Miles do continue to keep the poor house for £60 until Candalmas next. It is also ordered that overseers of the poor do at least once a week inspect the poor and report to the parish how the paupers therein are maintained in order that if there be any just complaint that the said Mr Miles may be properly spoke to and if necessary further dealt with and be turned out and the workhouse be let to another…"* In 1855 Elizabeth Herds aged 68 described as *"a pauper, of Eardisland"*, but living in Lyonshall, received weekly relief of two shillings.

The Old Post Office

228 It is believed that this is a late 16th century building, which has undergone much renovation over the centuries.

It is the end building of the three which has, at various times, housed a garage with petrol pumps (1929-83), a taxi service (set up by Rees Williams and Tommy Rimmer) and most recently a village stores and post office. This closed in 1990.

The former petrol station

229. This photograph dates from 1929 and shows the garage in use

The petrol station operated first under the direction of Mr Gransmore. He also provided a car repair service. One villager recalled that he would come out at night with a candle when someone wanted petrol and stick it in the pump in order to see what he was doing. The spot on which stands a large copper beech tree is believed to be the site of the old village work house.

The Burcott

230. The middle cottage of three

The whole is thought once to have been a yeoman's house, dating from the late 16th century. On the left hand side facing them can be seen the remains of a large bake house. There have been some alterations in the centuries since to each of the properties.

Apple Tree Cottage

231. The end cottage of the three, whose timbers are thought to date from about 1588.

The stone bake oven can be seen from the exterior, suggesting that it may once have been the village bakery. There is also an attractive inglenook fireplace in the property.

232. The three properties seen in the 1930s. A petrol pump can be seen outside the last of them when it was a garage

Orchard Green and the imitation Dovecote

233. These properties were built in 1986 by Border Oak. They were also designed to meet local needs and were then sold at between £35,000-£55,000.

The first home on the extreme left of the picture was that of local author, the late Paddy Ariss, who wrote many books, including 'Herefordshire Privies' here. There is a suggestion from a one time resident of Eardisland, Peggy Olausen (now in New Zealand), that a row of old cottages may once have stood on this site called Butcher's Row, which burnt down around the time of the first war. The tithe map (1842) shows such buildings existed closer to the road.

The small "village green" and Dovecote (which is purely decorative) accommodates the filtration system for the drainage treatment plan. It is based loosely on the one at Luntley.

234. Peter Ariss outside his home

The Elms

235. Originally a three bay timber framed building and probably thatched, the property was known as the Tan House in 1749 and Tan House farm by 1876.

The status of the owner is noted by the fact that in May 1749 they were granted Pew No 3 in the church. In 1865 the farmer living there was William Ensol, in 1875 it was William Matthews. In 1885 it was home to John Morris and in 1901 Philip Turner was farming until the time of the first war. It is not certain when the tannery was abandoned, but whilst it operated copious quantities of water were required in the tanning process. Early maps do indicate the existence of three pools fed by the millstream, together with a range of outbuildings, in the lower field, adjacent to the property. The pools have long since been filled in and the buildings demolished, conceivably part of the tanning activity. The house underwent major reconstruction in the late 19th, early 20th century when James Page, a builder from Leominster was commissioned to build a substantial extension in distinctive yellow bricks, together with a parapet walls to the original timber framed building in

236. Actress Maggie Smith was a guest here in the 1990s

the same style, and using the same brick type, along both the Bargates and the Hereford Road in Leominster. More latterly the elm trees behind the house were felled in the 1940s, when it was the home of Mr Watkins, a senior member of the Home Guard.

The Elms was operated as a working farm, under various ownership, until the late 1990s when Miss Johnson, the then owner, disposed of much of the remaining land and operated a Bed and Breakfast and touring caravan and campsite from the property. Maggie Smith, the Oscar winning actress, was a guest at the B & B in the early 1990s. The house is currently a private residence with the few remaining acres let for grazing.

Earlslaen House

237. An unusual house built from an early 15th century cruck frame barn

This unusual house is essentially an early 15th century cruck frame barn that was dismantled and re-erected in 1979-80. The barn was previously situated at Hay on Wye and when found was about to be destroyed and replaced with a steel framed cattle shed. The beams were so long they couldn't be transported by a lorry, they had to be cut. A condition of the Planning Approval was that an annex be erected to compliment the barn and the Conservation Officer insisted that the possibility of traditional oak framing be explored. So much interest was shown in the frame that the owner decided to start a small business, called Border Oak, which has subsequently become internationally famous. The roof of the building has 100 tonnes of traditional Herefordshire diminishing course stone tiles which took 9 months to complete.

Glebe Cottages

238.

These properties stand on the site of an old black and white house which was pulled down in the early 1970s. They were also Border Oak constructions and were built to a traditional plan and designed to be "affordable" local housing, selling at that time between £10,000-£16,000.

239. Alison and Richard Spoors outside their home.

240.

Knapp House

241. Knapp House, 2005

The Royal Commission on Historical Monuments of 1934 states that "*Knapp House is part of a 14th or early 15th century building, (a Hall house) to which an addition has been made on the South side, probably in the 16th century; this and the adjoining bay of the original building were heightened in the 18th century…*" As a cruck hall with two wings, later of two floors, it was probably originally open to the roof. Before the last war it was the home of the village undertaker and wheelwright. (In Victorian times it is thought to have been used as a blacksmith Shop). The back garden had a well and pump outside the back door and as in so may residences of the time, a hen run and pig sty. It fell into disrepair and was renovated in the early 1970s, which included rebuilding both bays at each end of the house and providing an entrance porch.

242. The Knapp House is one of the oldest buildings in the village. It is seen as it was in the 1930s from the back garden.

It is believed to be one of the oldest properties in the village and may have been a crude Wayside Inn when it was necessary to ford the river. It has the original truss which was located to one side of the cross passage.

There are one or two substantial decorated base cruck frames and there is evidence of smoke blackening to base cruck and rafters. It is interesting to note that also in the Parish is 'Knapp Orchard'. "Knapp" is quite a common field name in Herefordshire. The SMR (Sites and Monuments Register) lists 21 entries . Ekwall, "*The Concise Oxford Dictionary of English Place Names*" does not include any reference to Herefordshire but under Hampshire ascribes a "Knapp" to an Old English (Anglo-Saxon) root "*cnapp; top, mountain top.*" It may also have the meaning of "*small hill*". None of these seem relevant to our Knapp House, which may have received its name for some other reason. On the other hand it may be significant for other similarly named places in Herefordshire, even perhaps to "Knapp Orchard" in Lower Burton which is on a hill-side.

Shop Cottage, Shop House and Olde Shop House

These properties have been subject to major renovation in recent years,. This building in the centre of the village was a shop until 1983 and had been known as Stead's Shop since about 1905. It sold groceries, hand sliced bacon and cheese by the slab and everything from corn to paraffin. This property has remained in the same family for nearly 100 years. Olde Shop House was later

243. The central section of what was once Stead's shop

244. Stead's shop seen in the 1950s

245. Mrs Stead in the 1960s in the shop doorway.

the post office. The renovations provided new information about of the building's true age.

246. Shop Cottage

247. Shop House and Olde Shop House

The significance of this building had been overlooked by all previous experts until its exceptionally early construction was identified by Duncan James in 2005. His examination and analysis of its structure, suggests that it may date from late 14th or early 15th century. (1350-1450). This means that the building may be one of the oldest domestic properties known in Eardisland.

248. Malcolm and Cathy Dyer outside their home

It is one of only two cruck frames that have so far been identified in the village (the other is Knapp House, on the opposite of the road). This important discovery makes the building of special importance and interest. The house was renovated in 1994 when a fine stone fireplace (18th century) was uncovered together with some cruck and carved beams, including a rarely found trefoil, which give the much earlier date of likely construction.

249. The trefoil in the roof of Shop Cottage, Shop House and Olde Shop House.

The Trefoil in Tretower Court, Brecon

250. The photograph of the roof of Tretower Court (described as one of the most interesting houses of the medieval period in Wales) gives some idea of what the roof of the Olde Shop property may once have been like.

The Tretower roof construction has been described as "*of the finest craftsmanship and of handsome design*". In the Eardisland house there are five trusses most of which are hidden by internal plaster; but some parts are visible and there is evidence of smoke blackening. The roof has been raised at the eaves to increase the height of the first floor and this was probably done in the 17th century.

The Bungalow

251. The longstanding home of Eric and Gill Richards, who have family connections with the parish dating back more than a hundred years

The Old Smithy

252. The Old Smithy was in use as a blacksmith shop in the memory of many older residents

254.

The Blacksmiths in the 1860s until the turn of the century were John Griffiths and William Parry. From 1901 until the 1920s it was Mr Morris who was also a cycle builder and a craftsman in wrought iron. Mr Rooke followed and it was in use as an active blacksmiths shop until the late1930s. It subsequently became a village meeting place for the WI, a 'Men's Club', the Rifle Club and it served as the HQ of the Home Guard during the war. It has also been a butcher's shop, a Red Cross store and a wool shop. It was converted into a private dwelling in the 1980s.

The White Swan

253. A late 17th century building with later additions.

The White Swan (1930s)

255.

In the lounge bar is an Elizabethan period fireplace. The linen fold panelling was bought from Garnstone castle when it was demolished in the 1950s. In 1858 the proprietor was James Bassett (also a village carpenter). In 1885 the publican was James Caldicott, (he was also the miller at the time) and in 1898 it was run by Walter Stinton. In 1901 William Yates had taken over. Shortly afterwards, in 1905 Mr Prothero took charge. His niece, Florrie Jenkins, seen in the photograph, lived locally to the age of 100. In recent years it has been the place in which the cricket team has met for meetings and where they retire to for teas and refreshments after a match. The Eardisland Bat which is played for each year hangs in the bar. The pub is reputed to have one of the village ghosts in a bedroom. It is also the pub in which the one time village fiddle player, Colin Cole, used to play. Now many other local musicians perform here, including members of the Village Band.

Arrow Barns

256. This building was erected in the 1970s as a furniture showroom and was converted into residential use in the 1990s.

Manor House

257. This property has been previously named Porch House and later Vulcan House. It was first referred to as Old Manor House is in the RCHM Report 1934

258.

In his "Record Book", the Reverend Birley, Vicar of Eardisland 1917-1934 referred to it as Porch House quoting a newspaper report that stated "*There is now*" (in 1829) "*growing at the Porch House in Eardisland, Herefordshire (the property of J.P. Taylor Esq.,) a remarkably large and flourishing walnut tree…circumference of the trunk 12feet, height 66feet. The tree is so thickly covered with fruit that it is unable to sustain the ponderous load, so that branches are breaking. The whole crop may amount to at least four wagon loads.*" It was built in the first half of the 17th century (the central door is thought to be original, with ornamental strap hinges) on an L-shaped plan with the wings extending towards the north west and south west. Late in the same century the north west wing was extended and heightened and in the 18th century a brick extension was made on the south east front. The entrance has a C20th gabled porch. Between 1745 and 1778 Porch House was the residence of the Trumper family. The Will of John Trumper (dated 17th September 1745) bequeathed the property to his wife and assigns. On the passing of the great Reform Bill in 1832 it is reported that "*in the evening a general illumination took place in which the Porch House was shone conspicuous*".

Whilst called the Porch House it is recorded that there was a small dame school on the premises (the Dovecote) run by Mrs Parry. In 1878 the village teacher complained to the Inspectors that too many children were attending her school rather than his! In 1888, a village blacksmith, John Phillips lived there. In 1905 George Parry is described as '*a farmer, assistant overseer and collector of income tax and parish clerk*' was living there. In the 1920s, Albert Morris, the blacksmith was the owner when is was also known as Vulcan House. It was run as a guest house from 1930s by Mrs Rimmer and has continued to be so in recent times. This property is also reputed to have one of the several village ghosts. The village Dovecote was once part of this estate, but it was donated to the village in the late 1990s by the owner.

Adlen House

259. This property was the village post office from 1914-54

260. Adlen House from the main road.

It was the home of the village school teacher Mrs Davies and her family from 1914. Her husband was the village postmaster from that date until 1954. For many years the telephone exchange was here (the telephone number was 1). The kiosk was in place in 1947. The property remained as a gift shop until 1980. Megan Davies, one of their daughters, scored for the cricket team in the 1930s and played hockey for the county.

The Cross Inn

261.

262.

This is an 18th century building. In the 1870s when the Burton Court Cricket Club was getting established, the team repaired to the Cross for lunch. "*At two o'clock dinner was announced and then all adjourned to host Macklin's spread*". A Directory of 1902 states that Benjamin Goodenough, the publican, provided "*good accommodation for anglers and one and a half miles of private trout and grayling stream. Stabling, Arnold Perrets Gold Medal Ales and Stouts, the City Brewery Hereford. Price lists on application.*" In 1898 the publican was Elizabeth Cross, and in 1905 Josiah March; Benjamin Goodenough returned in 1908. In 1913 it was run by Edward Speke and in the 1920s by Albert Imms when it served as changing accommodation for footballers and the place in which they had their teas and refreshments. George Kay was the publican in the 1930s and 40s. It has become the meeting place of the airgun club in recent times.

Mill Stream Cottage

263. In the 1920s, Mr Dale, a partially disabled man lived here. Mrs Clowes provided him with work, keeping a pathway cleared from Burton Court to the church.

Bridge Cottage

This was formerly the old Grammar School and the Village Reading Room

264. The property in 2005

In 1603 William Whittington (of Street Court) made a bequest in his will. This stated *"I bequeath and give all that my portion of tithe in Street in the Parish of Kingsland for and towards the erection and maintenance of a Grammar School within the parish of Eardisland, and that the same to be erected."* The Headmaster was to be *"a learned, grave, and discreet scholar for ever to be chosen out of the universities of Oxford or Cambridge."* However, the school was not built until 1652, since the vicar of Kingsland had misappropriated the tithes. He was ordered to pay £78 in compensation. It remained the only school for the education of boys until about 1825, when a new school was built (now the Village Hall).

265. Col Clowes and his son talking to someone on the balcony steps of the Reading Room in 1905

The whipping post

266. The whipping post attached to the building can still be seen and relates back to the days when it was a school

267. The manacles of the whipping post

69

268. The old grammar school fell into disrepair but was renovated in 1888, by Mr Bassett of the village. It was let at a rent of one shilling a week

In 1870 it was used to educate a small number of girls, who moved on to the elementary school (now the village hall) in 1872. It was then purchased by John Clowes of Burton Court for £35, plus a piece of land on which a school master's house could be built. The upper part of the old grammar school became a Reading Room and meeting place. It was open every day (except for religious holidays) from 9am-9.30pm. Among the rules laid down in November 1872 were that it was under the management of the vicar and a small committee. Members paid one penny a week (non members paid one penny a visit). "*No publication of an infidel or immoral character shall be admissible; all newspapers and books to be submitted to the committee for approval.*" Provision was made to play chess, draughts and dominoes, but no games of chance and no betting was permitted. There was to be no loud talking; smoking was allowed to any member over the age of 18 on alternate days of the week. It continued to serve this purpose until 1936 when it was converted into a private residence.

River Cottage

269. This was the home of Nurse Goulter from 1909 for over 30 years.

She was appointed by Mrs Clowes who presented her with a long service medal in 1917. In 1931 the Kingsland Nursing Association agreed to share the costs of the Eardisland nurse (at £40p.a.). In the times of floods, she was seen to open the front door and enable the waters to rush straight through the back.

Folly farm

270. It is believed the property was built between about 1810-1820

It remains serviced by a reliable well 36 feet deep. It has a two roomed cellar one of which is tunnel construction of brick. Leslie Evans recalls taking 200 gallons of the Perry that he had made from the Folly Pears into the cellars in 1941. The resident there in 1858 was William Tomkins; in 1868 it was William Matthews. In 1875 Thomas James was farming there and in 1885 George Pullen. William and Thomas Hatfield followed until about 1905. In that year the farmer was John Prosser. He remained until the 1940s. Archaeologists recently working in the vicinity of Folly Farm have dated local river terracing to AD 50-250, evidencing that "*this unit formed part of the active flood plain during Roman times*". In the nearby field called Weir Patch there was, at beginning of the 20th century a short-lived fishery. All that remains is the weir on the river channel. In the 1930s gangs of men, known as "cloggers" arrived from Lancashire working in fields in Broome lane, opposite Folly farm. They came to cut alders which they trimmed and shaped into the thick soles of clogs. They were for use by the mill workers in and around Manchester. Many lodged in the village until their work for the season was completed.

Little Folly

271. This 17th century building was part of the Folly farm estate.

Wisteria Cottage

272. The property, formerly named Woodford, was built by Bob Prosser, in the 1940s having retired from work at Folly Farm.

273. The garden of Wisteria Cottage

The Ford

274. Where the children of the village learnt to swim prior to the bridging of the ford.

It was even used by people to wash their cars. There were occasions when those trying to cycle through came to grief in the slippery waters. It was a favourite meeting place for youngsters in summer.

Heybridge Farm

275. The property has timbers which were cut in a saw pit, suggesting it dates from at least the 17th century.

It was formerly known as The Cott. It was the home of the Drinkwater family in the 1920s and after the war, Sam and Mary Pugh farmed the land around it. The nearby bridge over the ford was built by Harold Davies (Roads and Bridges Engineer for Hereford). They were followed by the Blatchfords.

Broom Lane Cottage

276. An 18th century cottage.

The property was once owned by the Levick family and later the Corfields. They were followed by the Francis family, and then Cpt Bowler and his wife (who was Secretary of the PCC). After them, more recently, came the Savage family.

Riversdale

277. The main house dates to 1904; but the half timbered barn which adjoins it was formerly the village laundry and dates from the late 16th or early 17th century.

278. The Edwardian house was built to replace an earlier half timbered traditional black and white house (highlighted) which burnt down.

In 1901 Mrs Swayne occupied the property and in 1905, Henry Brigden was there until the Levick family purchased it in the 1920s. The property is marked on the Tithe map (1840-42) as *Seaside* (the origin of which is hard to unravel). It is thought that it was also once known as *Sunnyside* and was enlarged and extended by the Levick family. Mr Levick established the village fisheries which operated for some time and he also instituted the Levick Cup for the local football league in which the Eardisland Club played. Cup finals were played in Eardisland, although the cup has subsequently disappeared. Eardisland FC folded just before the war.

Arrow Lawn (2005)

279. It is thought to have been built in the 18th century except for the west range, which is 17th century.

It was formerly of two storeys, but with upper floor removed. It was known as "*New House*" in 1814 and later it was known for a time as the "*White House*". It is reputed to have had the first water closet in the village. The first recorded tenure is by the Haywood family in 1811. The status of the owner is noted by the fact that in 1814 they were granted Pew No 4 in the church. The ownership of the property had moved by marriage and inheritance to the Blackmore family by 1846. It was then the home of the Baptist Minister, Rev. Samuel Blackmore. At that date there was a cottage by the river

280. Arrow Lawn (highlighted) in 1900.

which was purchased, pulled down and laid out to garden; and at the same time the upper storey at the back of the house was added and the water closet installed.

In 1922 Mr Rupert Brooke was living in the property. Mr Samuel Blackmore, a retired tea planter, who owned it, bequeathed to the vicar the sum of £200 upon trust to invest and distribute the yearly income amongst the poor inhabitants of the parish. There is a thatched cider mill in the garden.

Arrow Lawn Cottage

281. A 17th century building which housed some evacuees during the war

Arrow Lawn Cottage was once occupied, in the 1920s, by the head gardener John Powell. During the second war Arrow Lawn was occupied by Mr and Mrs Richards, from London. They took in two evacuees from Bootle, June Somerset and Maureen Jenkinson. The barn was used as a beautiful music room in which the evacuees were encouraged to use the piano.

Upper Mill

282. A view from 1930s.

An indenture dated 15th May 1598 between Roger Vaughan (Lord of the Manor of Eardisland) and Nicholas Deyas, granted it to Deyas for the sum of £50 ("*of good lawful money*") for a term of 1000 years. An annual rent of 40 shillings was to be paid to Roger Vaughan at the

feast of St Michael the Archangel and the Annunciation. The lease also included rights to both banks of the mill leet right up to the weir. This was to ensure there was no interference with the water flow to the mill when it was working. An indenture of 1704 showed that Mr Phillips purchased the 500 year lease for £105. Edward, was a yeoman, was in business on his own account and ran the mill, until his death in 1710. Thomas Phillips, his son, was born and baptised in Eardisland in 1695; he died in 1773. His family continued to run the mill, (his wife died in 1785, aged 88). She was Hannah Walle, born in Eardisland in 1696. It would appear that the Upper Mill was owned by the Trumper family (Edward Phillips and Thomas Trumper were co-signatories as Churchwardens to the Parish register in 1697).

The will of John Trumper of Leene in Pembridge dated 17th September 1745, stated "*unto my loving wife Anne all that my water corn Grist Mill now in possession of Thomas Phillips situate in Eardisland in the said County with the gardens, fields, Backsides orchards, Summer House lands millstreams fishings fishponds Buildings Rights Members and Appurtenances thereunto belonging…*". The Phillips family continued to operate the mill, since in April 1831 George Davies was sentenced to transportation for life "*for stealing from Mr J. Phillips a quantity of wheat in a bag (and having previously been convicted on a felony)*". May Willett was also sentenced to 14 years transportation for receiving the same wheat, knowing it to have been stolen. It is remarkable to find that the Phillips family still have close connections with the area.

283. The ancient mill burnt down in the 1960s, but it has a long history. Domesday Book (1086) records two mills at Eardisland worth twenty-five shillings. This may have been one, the other was probably Glan Arrow Mill. Further research is in hand

The mill was an important feature of the local economy and was well used by local farmers. The prosperity of the surrounding area relied on its operation; in addition to grinding corn it also contained a grist mill that produced fodder for horses and cattle. It is doubtful that the millers lived on the premises, since it was noisy and dusty, and the frequency with which the names of the millers changes, suggests that they moved from one to another when required. In 1858 the miller was George Hancocks, in 1865 it was Thomas Coleshill and in 1905 Thomas George. In the 1920s the miller was Charlie Thomas, when it was also used to make cider. He lived in Staick Cottage, but there was an unusual occupant. John Davies, known as Ranter Jack, lived in the mill. He relied on the help of locals for survival, until his eyesight failed and he was taken to live in care in Weobley. This mill was grinding corn until the 1950s. In the war years it was used as a store for grain and cattle cake.

Mill House

284. This was built on the site of the Upper Mill which burnt down in the 1960s.

It became the home of a relative of a miller who occupied the mill in the 16th century. There are still features of the old mill within the property and it from here that the annual (plastic) duck race begins, each year.

The Dovecote

1469 is the year of the earliest reference to a dovecote at Eardisland (*Erleslane*) although it is likely that at least one dated to a very much earlier time than that. One of these is probably the one which was still standing in 1850 at Court House of which an illustration is extant (286).

The present brick building, renovated in 2000, was formerly part of the Manor House estate. This was previously known as the Porch House, as mentioned in the Will of John Trumper dated 17th September 1745. In 1934 the RCHM described the present building as… "*a square brick building, gabled on each face and with a square central lantern and weather vane; it is*

285. This is thought to be a late 17th or early 18th century building. It fell into disrepair and was beautifully renovated in 2000

probably of late 17th or early 18th century date. Condition-Good." This is now a Grade 2 listed building. A survey

286. A sketch of the old pigeon loft/dovecote which once stood near Court House.

in 1978 found that inside there are believed to be nearly 900 holes in the upper loft. These are arranged in vertical rows, each hole with a projecting semi-circular brick ledge. A Dovecote such as this was originally built as a source of food for the owner, probably the lord of the manor. It is thought that in the 17th century there were more than 16,000 in England alone. In 1893 at least 108 Dovecotes still existed in Herefordshire. There is evidence that this particular Dovecote also had a history as a school for girls in the late 19th century, before they were allowed to join the boys in the National School. The note book of Revd. Barker dated January 1869 states: "*J Clowes, having obtained from Mrs Parry of 12 Grove Lane that lower part of that picturesque old building attached to the Porch House and having put in good repair, he fitted it out as a school room at the cost to himself of £25*". Books were given by the vicar and Eardisland Girls school commenced on Monday January 8th 1869. There is a small fireplace in the room and coal was obtained from Mr Bassett and Mr Hornsby; the cost of one hundred weight was one shilling (5p). Mrs Leigh, the teacher, was paid a salary of £3 15shillings (£3.75) a quarter, (just over £1 a month).

The building underwent extensive renovations in 2000 having been donated to the village by the owner of the Manor House. It was opened to the public where the internal structure can be observed together with various exhibitions relating to village history. It is looked after by the village Dovecote Trust.

Bridge House and 1 Arrow Cottage

287. This property was once the village laundry

Old photographs show that this was a black and white timber framed building. It was once the site of the **Eardisland Laundry**. Advertisements appeared in the Leominster Journal at the time of the first world war, indicating that it was operating at the back of 'Bridge House'. Evidence of the large water pipes were found

during renovations. The Tithe map (1840/42) describes the property at the date of the mapping as "*house, building and old tan yard.*"

Bridgend

288. It was formerly Bridge Stores one of the two main shops in the village

The property is thought to date from the late 17th century; a mortgage document of 1805 suggests that the roof was raised at about that time. The frontage was bricked to cover the timber framing when it was no longer fashionable. The upper windows are late Victorian, early twentieth century additions and the frontage below followed between the wars. This was, for about 80 years, one of the important village stores.

It was first run, in the memories of the oldest villagers, by Mr Harvey. Before him it is thought to have been run by Mrs Caldicott. It sold household items, tinned food, overalls, stockings, vests, shoes as well as some groceries. Mr Harvey was the church organist for many years and instituted the cocoa concerts to raise funds for the daily cups of cocoa for children who could not get home for lunch from school. When it had the word *Accommodation* in bold letters across the frontage, it was said that every child in the Eardisland school could spell the word. The shop closed in the late 1960s, since when it has been a private residence.

289. The stores in the 1950s

75

Arrow Side

290. An elegant riverside house, once a farm building

This house was once a cowshed, and converted between the two wars. It has concrete floors to make it easier to deal with the flood water. In 1945 it was owned by Mr Smith who was a jeweller in Birmingham. He sold it to the Price family; the next owner was Fay Smith who subsequently sold it to Mr and Mrs Evans.

Arrow Cottage

291. An 17th century property which may once have been the third Eardisland pub, The Bull Inn

The property probably dates from between 1650-1680. Later, it may have been The Bull Inn. This is marked on the Tithe map (1841) by the river, east of the Nunhouse and a reference in a document indicates that it was used for vestry meetings in 1824. In the 1830s the children of John Baker, "a victualler of the Bull Inn" were christened. The pub is not shown on the 1851 census, although Thomas Bassett then lived at "*The Old Bull, near to the bridge*". At the back was a "*bull pen*" which was incorporated into the house in an extension built in the 1950s. Inside is an inglenook fireplace and a hook and ring can be seen in what was the bull pen. A correspondent, Mr Tanner, who spent his honeymoon in the property in 1943 recalls that the owner was Mrs Lewis, who had an undying admiration for Lawrence of Arabia. The cottage then had a hand pump above the kitchen sink and usual privy at the end of the garden.

Arrow Bank

292. It is thought that this may originally have been a black and white cottage dating from the 16th century (there are beams and Tudor bricks inside which indicate this).

Wattle and daub infill has been uncovered which shows how split staves are sprung into the oak beams. Lengths of wattle are woven across them. Plaster was applied, made from earth, lime and straw. It has subsequently been renovated and enlarged in almost every century since, so that its original L shape has been changed into its present dimensions. It is likely that a wealthy occupant made major changes in the 18th century, perhaps adding the elegant Georgian frontage. At the turn of the 20th century it was known as Arrow Villa and was the home of Mr and Mrs Henry Yeld. This family had long associations with Eardisland (see also p32). It is situated on what was in all probability once a drovers road; its stable block is now a garage. In very recent years the interior has been totally renovated by the present owners to restore it to an immaculate and elegant dwelling, also enjoyed by B & B visitors.

View towards the bridge 1900

293.

View to the bridge, 2005

294. These show the same view over a hundred year period. It is clear that the gardens on the river bank have gone, but little else has changed.

An evacuee, Margaret Collier, described how she returned to Eardisland in 1996 with her husband. As they set off for home, the last picture she had was of several village girls and boys sitting on the edge of the bridge in exactly the place where she used to sit with her friends about 56 years before.

Arrow Green

295. Erected in the 1960s, on the site of the old bowling green.

296. A scheduled ancient monument, (No 97) although its exact use remains something of a mystery.

The Mound in Monks Court

It is protected from any form of ground disturbance including metal detecting. The name suggests that it may have had an association with a monastic house, perhaps Limebrook Priory or Wigmore Abbey. It is probably the place where the court leet was held in the days when tithes were paid to them. In the course of the Eardisland Feast in 1826 it is recorded that there was a performing company which acted in the Tithe Barn at Monks Court for 5 nights. One of the pieces they performed was "Bluebeard". The circular mound is 31 yards at the base rising to 1.5m above the surrounding ground.

297. Typical Tithe barn. Often the larger and older barns in an area may have served the purpose of being a Tithe Barn.

It was the custom as far back as Saxon times (pre-Norman Conquest) for the local church to receive a tenth of the crops grown by people in the parish and one in ten sheep, oxen or foals. This was the tithe. The place in which the gifted seasonal items were stored was the Tithe Barn. The size of the Barn may be an indication of the amount of the tithes received. The system fell out of use from about 1836, when the clergy began to receive a monetary payment in place of the crop. It is believed that such a Tithe Barn stood in Monks Court meadow.

The Sites & Monuments Record database suggests it is the reduced remains of a motte with faint traces of a ditch on northern side, but no evidence of a bailey. It may have been designed to raise the building above the flood plain. The Woolhope Club discussion paper suggested it may have been a siege castle, (being just out of range of a long bow from the moated motte close to the church on which a building may have stood), a religious holding, a fortified manor house or a temporary fortification before the construction of a larger castle.

In 1850 a farmer at Brockaley, near Broxwood (then in the parish) came to pay his tithes here. He arrived to find the river in flood. He hired a small boat and duly arrived at the court to make his payment. This indicates the significance of the site at that time. Local legend has it that the dip in the top of the mound suggests it was once the site for cock fighting. But there is no documentary evidence for this. However, the central area has sunk over the last 50 years. At one time before the war the grass could be cut using horses. This subsequently became impossible.

Monks Cottage

298, 299. These photographs show how the property has changed in a century

This property is marked on the Tithe map 1840-42 as plot 547 (house and garden). It is thought to have been built circa 1600 and was once thatched; the exterior gable beams indicate that the roof has been raised. The Victorian photograph shows how little the main structure of the house has changed in over 100 years.

By 1948 it was described as derelict and there was a demolition order in force in 1956, which was rescinded in 1958. It subsequently underwent major renovation work.

300. Monks Cottage 2005

Lime Cottage 2005

301. A 17th century cottage.

302. This photograph from the 1920s shows some of the changes which have taken place since.

This is thought to be a 17th century cottage which has been subject to additions in more recent times. In 1905 the occupant was Henry Harvey who was a poultry and egg dealer. He went on to become the proprietor of one of the village stores. In more recent times this was the home of the Claire and Bill Price. Bill was the Secretary of the Eardisland Cricket Club and its long time umpire, Claire was the Club scorer for many seasons.

Sectors 7 and 8
Lime Lane to Hinton Manor

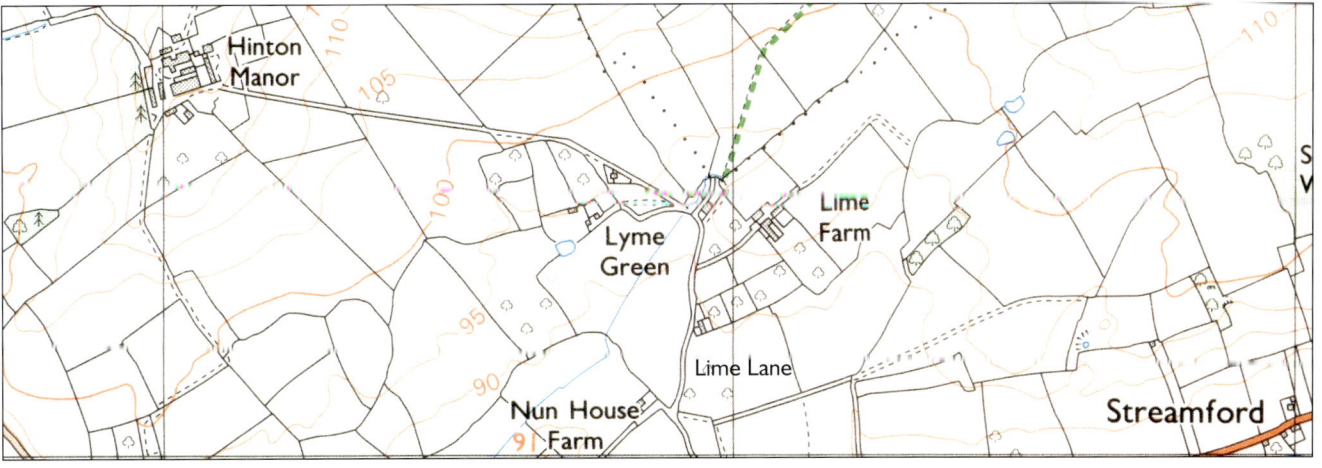

302. The map shows the area in which the properties appear in this section (7 & 8)

Lime lane

It is uncertain as to the origin of the name of the lane. The spelling of places and properties along it varies between Lime and Lyme. It is speculated that the name may have a connection with the agricultural use of Lime in the mid 17th century (which has been noted in Herefordshire at that time). At Hinton, it was recorded in 1772 & 1776, there were "*lands called Park Grounds with lime kilns thereon and 25 acres of woodland*". It could equally be associated with a plantation of lime trees. Another possibility is that the land on which the building stood was held by the priory of Limebrook (in Lingen). This was originally a Benedictine cell belonging to Avency in Normandy; there was also a priory of nuns, founded by some of the Mortimer family about the reign of Richard 1st (1189-1199). It was finally suppressed in 1553. But whilst it existed there was much land in the area from which tithes were gathered to support the nuns. It is probable that in the early 19th century many properties in this part of the village were owned by the Haywood family.

The Oaks

304.

305.

A post war property

79

Meadow Edge

306. The bungalow was built in 1960.

In 1965 it was known as Collingwood and later Conifers. Several significant additions have been made since that date.

The Nun House

307. There is little doubt that the name derives from the Nuns of Limebrook Priory who had a cell here and who were endowed with various lands in the parish of Eardisland

The earliest reference uncovered is to 1542 when it was spelt "Nonne House". A 1974 Woolhope Club paper on the subject of "*The Nunnery of Limebrook and its Property*" describes the Nun House as "*a very complicated building partly 18th century and probably 20th century stone and partly timber-framed of c.1600, but in the centre of the main block is a 12 ft. bay of what appears to be an earlier building. It is timber-framed and has a span of 12 ft. It is probably part of the medieval house now almost lost in later additions.*" Records show that during the latter part of the Victorian period, the Edwards

family were farming there in 1872 and James Stephens in 1885; in 1898 Philip Turner was the occupant (moving on to the Elms by 1902).

Tom Mainwaring undertook research into the history of the Nun House Farm, since he had lived there in the early part of the twentieth century. His family purchased the property in 1904 (having previously lived at Morcot Farm, Lyonshall). He recalled that in those early days, the main produce included wheat, oats, barley, root crops, swedes, potatoes as well as fruit. There were no chemical fertilisers available, slurry and manure were used. When necessary, ploughing was often undertaken on moonlit nights with hurricane lamps hung at strategic points in the fields. Straw was put through a chaffing machine, mangolds and swedes went through a chipping machine and were mixed with molasses or a dark coloured syrup obtained from sugar and fed to the stock. The farm house larder was always well stocked with sides of bacon and hams, home cured to feed the family through the winter. Cider and Perry was brewed (as it was at most farms) and old rum and port casks frequently used for storage. The wages of the farm workers was very low. In 1890 they earned on average about 9 shillings a week (45pence) and in 1935 about 35 shillings a week (£1.75p) Apart from cider, they did receive free milk, two rows of potatoes and one row of carrots and swedes. The cost of living was also quite different. In 1912 it was usual to buy 20 eggs for a shilling (5p); A pint of beer cost a few pence; a bullock cost about £2.10shillings (£2.50) Coal was £1. 2shillings a ton (£1.10p). However, in 1912 the farm suffered a severe attack of foot and mouth disease causing all the animals to be slaughtered. As a result, his father gave up farming and moved to Wellcote. The Nun House was sold to the Griffith family. John Griffiths died in 1943 and his son carried on running the farm. It finally changed hands again in 1992.

The Caravan Park

308. The caravan park developed in the 1970s. After the second war, the cricket club played on a pitch at the Nun House for about ten seasons.

Crabtree House

309. This may once have been a cider house, since it was on an ancient track way.

In 1905 John Davies was the occupant. In the 1920s it belonged to Street Court estate (the Patten family). At that time it had a thatched roof and was in a poor state of repair. The Watkins family then purchased it (for £375 with 5 acres) and undertook renovations. Peggy Olausen, who lived there recalls that there used to be a very old gnarled crab-apple tree beside the front door and a walnut tree in the back garden. There is a spring well in the orchard and another in the cellars which has never been known to go dry.

Lyme Cottage

310. A property thought to date from the early 17th century, which has undergone many changes in the years since.

A sale document of 1938 indicates it was two cottages at that time, probably for workers on one of the local estates.

Lyme Green farm

In the later part of the 19th. Century it is thought that this property was the home of Thomas Amos and his family. In 1875 he is described as 'a shoe maker' and in 1898 as 'the Parish Clerk'. From 1901 he is certainly in occupation of the property as a farmer, where he

311. A very old property which has been greatly modernised in very recent years.

remained until the 1920s. It was then farmed by Charles Powles and his family until recent times.

Lyme Green Cottages

312. Homes originally built to house workers on local estates

Hinton Bungalow

313. A property built to house workers on the estate

81

Hinton Manor

314. Peter and Zigi Davenport on the lawns of Hinton Manor, one of the four Manors of Eardisland

Hinton is one of the four Manors of Eardisland. There are several versions of the place name Hinton (there are at least four in Herefordshire). One of the accepted translations of the name is its derivation from Hean-Tun meaning a high-fortified place. The earliest reference to Hinton is dated 1190 in the Leominster Cartulary; here it appears as Hentun. The lordship of the manor from 1211 is quite well established for the following 322 years, at the end of which it is shown that Hinton was owned by Katherine of Aragon between 1533-35. In 1533 Cranmer declared the marriage of Henry 8th and Katherine to be invalid. She died at Kimbolton in Cambridgeshire in 1536 when her lands would have reverted to Royal control. There is nothing to indicate when the Crown divested itself of the Manor of Hinton, but in 1612, the Lord of the Manor was Richard Smith and the property thereafter passed through many hands. In 1858 Thomas Hall was the resident; Benjamin Sanders was owner between 1870-1900; then John Paton (1909-1926). It is thought that it was purchased by Mr Eckley in 1924 and sold by his son to Mrs Chapman in 1954. It was sold again by auction on 3rd July 1963.

314a.   The lands which form the Hinton Manor Estate.

Conclusions

What this photographic record shows is that something of the important heritage and history of Eardisland can be traced through its buildings and places of significance. The traditional building methods can still be seen in a few of the most ancient houses, some of which have only been revealed through the processes of renovation (see Olde Shop House, Shop House and Shop Cottage, p65). The use of oak construction has been reintroduced in several recent developments to maintain the traditions. The fact that few buildings exist from before about 1420 (except the church) suggests that the devastation which took place in the Marches in the early years of the 15th century with the exploits of Owen Glendower and his powerful opponents must also have affected Eardisland.

As it became more settled and rebuilding took place, the power transferred to local Lords of the Manor and a few large landowners. The majority of the oldest black and white buildings were erected to house their employees, who worked the land or provided other services. Many such properties retain the word Cott (Cot, Cote) in their name. The 'cottagers' of Eardisland are frequently referred to in documents. They even had special categories in which they could compete in local horticultural shows. In 1872 the parish magazine records *"Cottagers only: a collection of vegetables, not less than 5 useful varieties: prize three shillings"*. The fact that many owners of such buildings have few historical deeds for their properties indicates that theirs were part of an estate of a local landowner. A few which do exist, provide interesting insights into some of the other unchanging aspects of local history.

The deeds of Wellcote (see p34) show the largely unchanging monetary value of a small black and white cottage over about 150 years. In 1790 it was let at 4pence a year (as part of the Court House estate); in 1863 it was sold for £50; in 1899 for £55, and 1920 it was purchased for £70. Even in 1952 it was valued at just £400.

It is apparent that there had been considerable influxes of new wealth into the parish from time to time over many centuries. For example, Court

House deeds show that this property was purchased by Thomas Bennet (a citizen of London) in 1614; later he sold it to John Greene 'a salter' and Thomas Clee (a brewer), both of London. It is likely that similar processes took place after the Restoration, from 1660. The result no doubt being that many properties in the hands of wealthy individuals underwent considerable architectural change (see also the Burton Court and the Dingley drawing p19). However, the major changes in the social structure of the village in more recent times, as revealed in the properties we have recorded, seem to have come in the Victorian period and prior to the first war. At that time, there was a movement into the village of a wealthy class who built new substantial homes (such as Glan Arrow) or who improved and renovated older properties of some status. Burton Court had been subject to such changes from an earlier period as a result of its historical significance. The newcomers included a retired tea planter (at Arrow Lawn), a hard working vicar (in Staick House) and landowners from other parishes also took over local properties (such as Lynch Court).

After 1945 many old estates broke up and tenants purchased their properties; smallholdings merged into larger farms and there was an influx of newcomers to the village, many of whom renovated or expanded older properties. This process of home improvement has continued in recent years among larger numbers of home owners as property prices have escalated; a number of new houses have been built to meet the demand for properties in this beautiful village.

There has been a small growth in population in the parish (although comparisons are difficult over time as a result of boundary changes, it seems to be about the same in 2001 as in 1891). The time when it was largely self sufficient has passed; between the wars there were large numbers of smallholdings which have subsequently declined, with their land sold off to large farms. At the same time the village shops, garage, post office and schools have all changed their functions. Although these have been serious losses

315. Craftsman Roger Brookes carving a fish in his workshop at Burton Court

(especially the closure of the school) there have been benefits. There has been the growth in a thriving community, in which new occupational groups have emerged, including skilled craftsmen and women, working in wood, jewellery and ceramics, builders and decorators. Also, those businesses catering for the needs of tourists and passing visitors (as well as the local population). Apart from the tea rooms and farm shop, even Burton Court is opening its doors to Conferences and weddings. New publishing ventures have been established (including a lively parish magazine) and many authors live in this village as well as successful sports men and women. There have also developed groups which research the history of the parish. Others have emerged which work successfully for the renovation of buildings which might otherwise have fallen into decay, such as the Church and the 18th century Dovecote and the preservation of structures which are important parts of the local heritage, like the 1920s AA Box.

Eardisland has won many awards and plaudits for being such a beautiful and well tended village over the years. It was the winner of the Best Kept Village in Herefordshire (1954).

317. Prettiest Village Award (Central TV) 1987

316. Best Kept Village Award 1954

It was adjudged to be the Prettiest Village in Herefordshire (Central Television award) 1987. It was the winner of Village Pride award 2004. All this indicates the hard work and dedication of its inhabitants to the maintenance of the environment.

It is apparent that pride in its history and heritage will ensure the maintenance of its buildings into the future, although no doubt further changes will be recorded again at some time in the future, when perhaps this project is repeated.

318. Village Pride Award 2004

Sources and bibliography

Reference is made in describing some of the properties to RCHM: (The Royal Commission on Historical Monuments) 1934. This listed monuments that the Commissioners selected as especially worthy of preservation at that time.

The Leon Valley; Reeves, N. (Phillimore, 1980)

Eardisland Parish Magazines (1990-2005)

The Eardisland WI Book (1956)

Directories: Littlebury's & Kelly's (1865-1941)

History & Directory of Herefordshire (1858)

Woolhope papers

Eardisland: an oral history. Saxon Press (1995)

eardislandhistory.co.uk

The Arrow Valley, Herefordshire, K. Ray; P. White. Orphans Press (2003)

Herefordshire Past and Present, R. Richardson and C. Musson. Logaston Press (2004)

The Hereford Record Office

Ancient Monuments Vol. 4. C. Fox (1950)

Reports by Duncan James (2005)

The Hereford Times

Sites and Monuments Record (SMR) www.smr.herefordshire.gov.uk

Windmills in Shropshire Hereford & Worcester. Seaby & Smith 1983. Stevenage Museum Publications

Eardisland Dovecote. Dovecote Trust 2000

Acknowledgements and sources

This publication has been made possible by grant funding from The Local Heritage Initiative (LHI) administered by the Countryside Agency and funded by the Heritage Lottery Fund and Nationwide Building Society.

The members of the Eardisland Oral History Group who have compiled the information between 2000-2005 are Gill Richards, Pat Roche, Cathy Dyer, John and Jenny Gittoes, Brian and Tina Powell, Jane Watson and Paul Selfe. We are particularly grateful to Jane Watson who has provided the majority of the photographs for this project. We thank others, including Chris O'Grady, Graham Simpson, Barry Freeman and Chris Bivand for their contributions and the Hereford Times, who have supplied important photographs for our use and Ordnance Survey for permission to reproduce the maps.

We acknowledge the valuable help and suggestions for the text accompanying some of the photographs received from Duncan James (122, 208, 243) and George Alderson (who has spent many research hours in the Hereford Record Office and also in examining property deeds loaned by villagers).

We are also grateful for the information supplied by many of the property owners and those with detailed recollections of village social history, which has greatly assisted us. Any errors in the text are ours and will be amended in our files if we are informed of them.

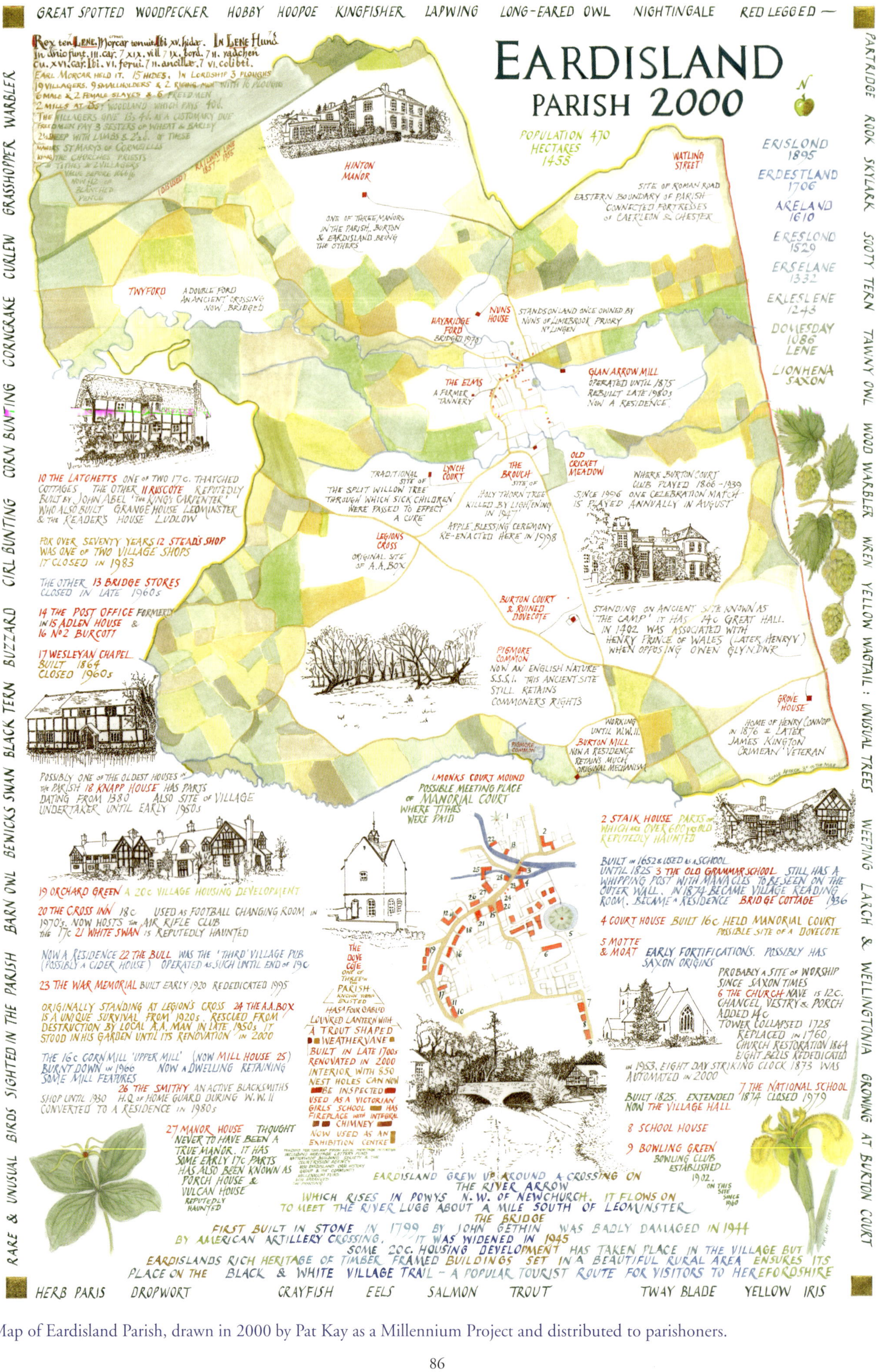
GREAT SPOTTED WOODPECKER HOBBY HOOPOE KINGFISHER LAPWING LONG-EARED OWL NIGHTINGALE RED LEGGED —
PARTRIDGE ROOK SKYLARK SOOTY TERN TAWNY OWL WOOD WARBLER WREN YELLOW WAGTAIL : UNUSUAL TREES WEEPING LARCH & WELLINGTONIA GROWING AT BURTON COURT
RARE & UNUSUAL BIRDS SIGHTED IN THE PARISH BARN OWL BEWICKS SWAN BLACK TERN BUZZARD CIRL BUNTING CORN BUNTING CORNCRAKE CURLEW GRASSHOPPER WARBLER
HERB PARIS DROPWORT CRAYFISH EELS SALMON TROUT TWAY BLADE YELLOW IRIS
EARDISLAND
PARISH 2000
N
Rex ten LENE. Morcar tenuit. Ibi xv. hidæ. In Lene Hund.
In dnio sunt. iii. car. 7 xix. vill 7 ix. bord. 7 ii. radchen
cu. xvi. car. Ibi. vi. serui. 7 ii. ancillæ. 7 vi. colibti.
EARL MORCAR HELD IT. 15 HIDES. IN LORDSHIP 3 PLOUGHS
19 VILLAGERS. 9 SMALLHOLDERS & 2 RIDING MEN WITH 16 PLOUGHS
6 MALE & 2 FEMALE SLAVES & 6 FREEDMEN
2 MILLS AT 15s; WOODLAND WHICH PAYS 40d.
THE VILLAGERS GIVE 13s 4d. AS A CUSTOMARY DUE
FREEDMEN PAY 3 SESTERS OF WHEAT & BARLEY
(DISUSED) RAILWAY LINE 1857 – 1955
POPULATION 470
HECTARES 1458
HINTON MANOR
ONE OF THREE MANORS IN THE PARISH.. BURTON & EARDISLAND BEING THE OTHERS
WATLING STREET
SITE OF ROMAN ROAD EASTERN BOUNDARY OF PARISH CONNECTED FORTRESSES OF CAERLEON & CHESTER
ERISLOND 1895
ERDESTLAND 1706
ARELAND 1610
ERESLOND 1529
ERSELANE 1332
ERLESLENE 1243
DOMESDAY 1086 LENE
LIONHENA SAXON
TWYFORD
A DOUBLE FORD AN ANCIENT CROSSING NOW BRIDGED
HAYBRIDGE FORD BRIDGED 1970
NUNS HOUSE
STANDS ON LAND ONCE OWNED BY NUNS OF LIMEBROOK PRIORY Nr LINGEN
GLAN ARROW MILL
OPERATED UNTIL 1875 REBUILT LATE 1980s NOW A RESIDENCE
THE ELMS
A FORMER TANNERY
LYNCH COURT
TRADITIONAL SITE OF THE SPLIT WILLOW TREE THROUGH WHICH SICK CHILDREN WERE PASSED TO EFFECT A CURE
THE BROUCH
SITE OF HOLY THORN TREE KILLED BY LIGHTENING IN 1947
APPLE BLESSING CEREMONY RE-ENACTED HERE IN 1998
OLD CRICKET MEADOW
WHERE BURTON COURT CLUB PLAYED 1866 – 1939
SINCE 1996 ONE CELEBRATION MATCH IS PLAYED ANNUALLY IN AUGUST
LEGIONS CROSS
ORIGINAL SITE OF A.A. BOX
BURTON COURT & RUINED DOVECOTE
STANDING ON ANCIENT SITE KNOWN AS 'THE CAMP' IT HAS 14c GREAT HALL. IN 1402 WAS ASSOCIATED WITH HENRY PRINCE OF WALES (LATER HENRY V) WHEN OPPOSING OWEN GLYNDWR
PIGMORE COMMON
NOW AN ENGLISH NATURE S.S.S.I. THIS ANCIENT SITE STILL RETAINS COMMONERS RIGHTS
PIGMORE COMMON
WORKING UNTIL W.W.II.
BURTON MILL
NOW A RESIDENCE RETAINS MUCH ORIGINAL MECHANISM
GROVE HOUSE
HOME OF HENRY CONNOP IN 1876 & LATER JAMES KINGTON CRIMEAN VETERAN
SCALE APPROX 3" TO THE MILE
10 THE LATCHETTS ONE OF TWO 17c. THATCHED COTTAGES THE OTHER 11 RUSCOTE REPUTEDLY BUILT BY JOHN ABEL 'THE KING'S CARPENTER' WHO ALSO BUILT GRANGE HOUSE LEOMINSTER & THE READER'S HOUSE LUDLOW
FOR OVER SEVENTY YEARS 12 STEAD'S SHOP WAS ONE OF TWO VILLAGE SHOPS IT CLOSED IN 1983
THE OTHER 13 BRIDGE STORES CLOSED IN LATE 1960s
14 THE POST OFFICE FORMERLY IN 15 ADLEN HOUSE & 16 No2 BURCOTT
17 WESLEYAN CHAPEL BUILT 1864 CLOSED 1960s
POSSIBLY ONE OF THE OLDEST HOUSES IN THE PARISH 18 KNAPP HOUSE HAS PARTS DATING FROM 1380 ALSO SITE OF VILLAGE UNDERTAKER UNTIL EARLY 1950s
19 ORCHARD GREEN A 20c VILLAGE HOUSING DEVELOPMENT
20 THE CROSS INN 18c USED AS FOOTBALL CHANGING ROOM IN 1970's. NOW HOSTS THE AIR RIFLE CLUB
THE 17c 21 WHITE SWAN IS REPUTEDLY HAUNTED
NOW A RESIDENCE 22 THE BULL WAS THE 'THIRD' VILLAGE PUB (POSSIBLY A CIDER HOUSE) OPERATED AS SUCH UNTIL END OF 19C
23 THE WAR MEMORIAL BUILT EARLY 1920 REDEDICATED 1995
ORIGINALLY STANDING AT LEGION'S CROSS 24 THE A.A. BOX IS A UNIQUE SURVIVAL FROM 1920s. RESCUED FROM DESTRUCTION BY LOCAL A.A. MAN IN LATE 1950s IT STOOD IN HIS GARDEN UNTIL ITS RENOVATION IN 2000
THE 16c CORN MILL 'UPPER MILL' (NOW MILL HOUSE 25) BURNT DOWN IN 1966 NOW A DWELLING RETAINING SOME MILL FEATURES
26 THE SMITHY AN ACTIVE BLACKSMITHS SHOP UNTIL 1930 H.Q OF HOME GUARD DURING W.W.II CONVERTED TO A RESIDENCE IN 1980s
27 MANOR HOUSE THOUGHT NEVER TO HAVE BEEN A TRUE MANOR. IT HAS SOME EARLY 17c PARTS HAS ALSO BEEN KNOWN AS PORCH HOUSE & VULCAN HOUSE REPUTEDLY HAUNTED
1. MONKS COURT MOUND POSSIBLE MEETING PLACE OF MANORIAL COURT WHERE TITHES WERE PAID
THE DOVE COTE ONE OF THREE IN THE PARISH KNOWN TO HAVE EXISTED HAS A FOUR GABLED LOUVRED LANTERN WITH A TROUT SHAPED WEATHERVANE BUILT IN LATE 1700s RENOVATED IN 2000 INTERIOR WITH 850 NEST HOLES CAN NOW BE INSPECTED USED AS A VICTORIAN GIRLS SCHOOL HAS FIREPLACE WITH INTEGRAL CHIMNEY NOW USED AS AN EXHIBITION CENTRE
2 STAIK HOUSE PARTS OF WHICH ARE OVER 600 YRS OLD REPUTEDLY HAUNTED
BUILT IN 1652 & USED AS A SCHOOL UNTIL 1825 3 THE OLD GRAMMAR SCHOOL STILL HAS A WHIPPING POST WITH MANACLES TO BE SEEN ON THE OUTER WALL. IN 1874 BECAME VILLAGE READING ROOM. BECAME A RESIDENCE BRIDGE COTTAGE 1936
4 COURT HOUSE BUILT 16c HELD MANORIAL COURT POSSIBLE SITE OF A DOVECOTE
5 MOTTE & MOAT EARLY FORTIFICATIONS. POSSIBLY HAS SAXON ORIGINS
PROBABLY A SITE OF WORSHIP SINCE SAXON TIMES 6 THE CHURCH NAVE IS 12C. CHANCEL, VESTRY & PORCH ADDED 14c TOWER COLLAPSED 1728 REPLACED IN 1760 CHURCH RESTORATION 1864 EIGHT BELLS REDEDICATED IN 1953. EIGHT DAY STRIKING CLOCK 1873 WAS AUTOMATED IN 2000
7 THE NATIONAL SCHOOL BUILT 1825. EXTENDED 1874 CLOSED 1979 NOW THE VILLAGE HALL
8 SCHOOL HOUSE
9 BOWLING GREEN BOWLING CLUB ESTABLISHED 1902. ON THIS SITE SINCE 1960
EARDISLAND GREW UP AROUND A CROSSING ON THE RIVER ARROW WHICH RISES IN POWYS N.W. OF NEWCHURCH. IT FLOWS ON TO MEET THE RIVER LUGG ABOUT A MILE SOUTH OF LEOMINSTER
THE BRIDGE FIRST BUILT IN STONE IN 1799 BY JOHN GETHIN WAS BADLY DAMAGED IN 1944 BY AMERICAN ARTILLERY CROSSING. IT WAS WIDENED IN 1945
SOME 20c. HOUSING DEVELOPMENT HAS TAKEN PLACE IN THE VILLAGE BUT EARDISLANDS RICH HERITAGE OF TIMBER FRAMED BUILDINGS SET IN A BEAUTIFUL RURAL AREA ENSURES ITS PLACE ON THE BLACK & WHITE VILLAGE TRAIL – A POPULAR TOURIST ROUTE FOR VISITORS TO HEREFORDSHIRE

Map of Eardisland Parish, drawn in 2000 by Pat Kay as a Millennium Project and distributed to parishoners.

The Village looking northwest

In the left foreground is the Village Hall (up to 1979 it was the Village School). Left of that are the recreation Ground and Bowling Green. The Parish Church is in the centre, with the trees on the Saxon motte to the right, in shadow. Beyond the trees are houses on the banks of the River Arrow. On the village outskirts is Arrow Bank Caravan Park and across the top of the picture is the slope of the northern side of the Arrow Valley.

St Mary's Walk

Built in 1998–99 on part of a village centre farmyard, the 13 new houses are integrated with former farm buildings which have since been skillfully converted into dwellings. Parts of these buildings are seen on the right, including a redundant hop kiln. Our main historic feature, the Saxon Moat, is lower left and the trees are growing on the central motte. The nearby church tower can just be seen in the top left corner.

The front cover shows **The Village looking northeast**

Here we see part of the main village street leading to the bridge across the River Arrow. The Dovecote is to the left of the car and the river can be seen between the houses. The long building in the lower centre is modern but faced in traditional style. The red brick building is the former Blacksmith's and the two public houses are in the right hand corner.

All aerial photographs are reproduced by permission.

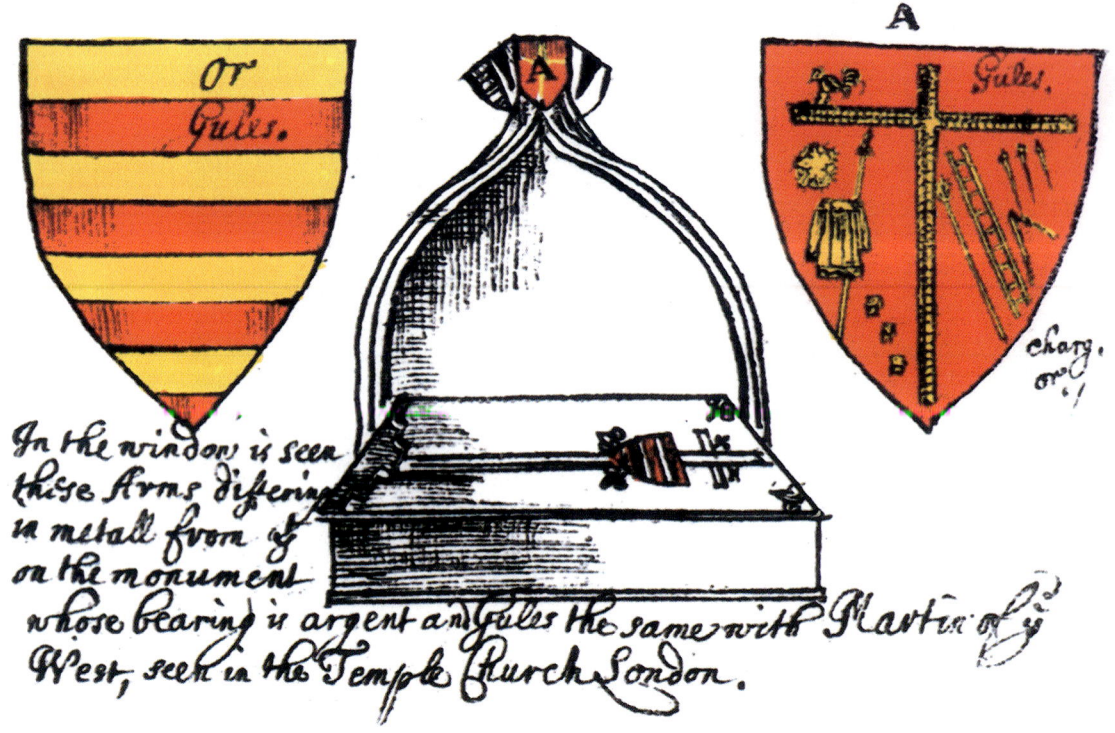

Here is little of Antiquity except this monument adjoining to the wall of the seat of Mr Brewster of Burton without Inscription, on the top onely are seen y coats following and the Device marked A

Or
Gules.

A
Gules.
charg. or.

In the window is seen these Arms differing in metall from y on the monument whose bearing is argent and Gules the same with Martin of y West, seen in the Temple Church London.

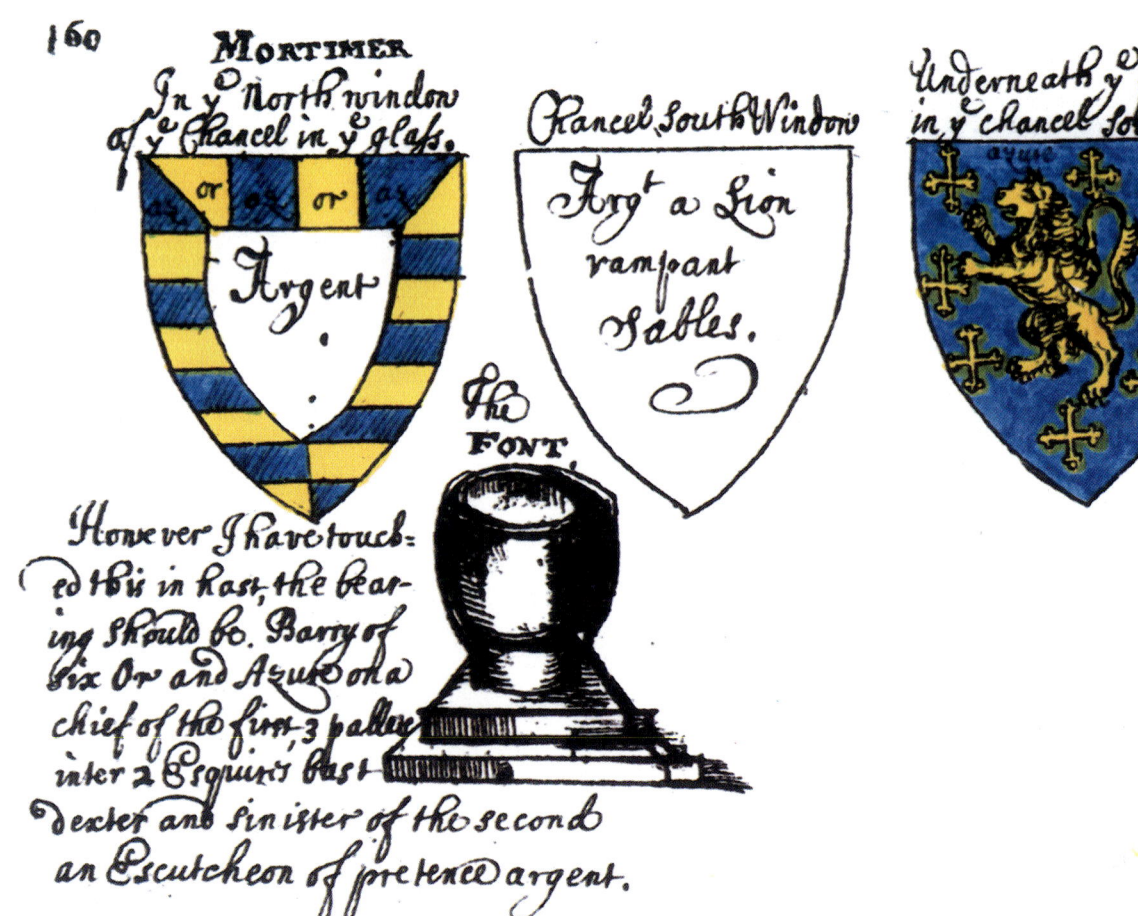

160

MORTIMER
In y North window of y Chancel in y glass.
or az or az
Argent

Chancel South Window
Arg t a Lion rampant Sables.

Underneath y former in y chancel south glass.
azure

THE FONT

However I have touch: ed this in hast, the bearing should be. Barry of Six Or and Azure on a chief of the first 3 pallets inter 2 Esquire's hast dexter and sinister of the second an Escutcheon of pretence argent.

Eardisland Church: details of the tomb canopy, the font and other heraldry.
Painted from the original pen and ink drawings by Thomas Dingley circa 1683.

88

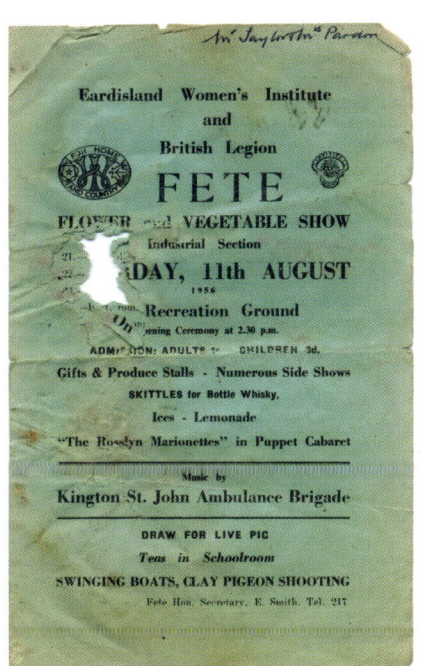

Eardisland Village Show 2003

Eardisland Village Hall
Saturday 23rd August

2pm - 4.30pm
(presentation of awards 4.15pm)

Refreshments
Raffle
Show Entries

Admission
Adults 50p ~ Under 16s FREE

sponsored by
Eardisland Community Millennium Fund

Programmes for the Village Show, 1954, 1956 and 2003

HEREFORDSHIRE

Village of Eardisland

Russell, Baldwin & Bright, Ltd.

are instructed to SELL BY AUCTION, at

The Royal Oak Hotel, Leominster

ON

FRIDAY, MAY 16th, 1947

At 3 p.m.

The Picturesque half-timbered Cottage

KNOWN AS

"ORCHARD COTTAGE"

Constructed of brick and half timber with an excellent roof half slate and half tile and containing Living Room, large Pantry, Two Bedrooms, Back Kitchen, Wash House, Coal and Wood Shed, Pigs Cot.

Good Garden. Small Plot of Land at rear of Cottage. Pump Water Supply.

The Property is most pleasantly situated facing south in the charming village of Eardisland which is famous as a beauty spot, and the daily bus service from Kington to Leominster passes the property.

Lugg Drainage Rate 11s. 2d.

A Strip of Land which comprises the ditch and an additional one yard in width along the whole of the frontage is to be dedicated to the public as part of the public highway when the authorities shall require it, upon terms that there will be no charge against the property for roadmaking, paving, etc., and the Council will also plant a new hedge along the new frontage line.

VACANT POSSESSION will be given on completion of the purchase.

To view, apply: Mr. T. G. SMITH, West End, Eardisland.

Further particulars from the Solicitor, Mr. J. H. COOPER, West Street, Leominster; or the AUCTIONEERS, Leominster, Hereford and Tenbury Wells.

LEOMINSTER PRINTING CO., LTD.

Notice of auction sale in 1947.

List of Illustrations

Index